What If We Taught the Way Children Learn?

For Patti Page, whose friendship these many years has been a blessing and a joy. So many memories!

What If We Taught the Way Children Learn?

More Straight Talk About Bettering Education and Children's Lives

Rae Pica

A SAGE Publishing Company

FOR INFORMATION:

Corwin

A SAGE Company

2455 Teller Road

Thousand Oaks, California 91320

(800) 233-9936

www.corwin.com

SAGE Publications Ltd.

1 Oliver's Yard

55 City Road

London EC1Y 1SP

United Kingdom

SAGE Publications India Pvt. Ltd.

B 1/I 1 Mohan Cooperative Industrial Area

Mathura Road, New Delhi 110 044

India

SAGE Publications Asia-Pacific Pte. Ltd.

18 Cross Street #10-10/11/12

China Square Central

Singapore 048423

Publisher: Jessica Allan

Senior Content Development Editor: Lucas Schleicher

Associate Content Development Editor: Mia Rodriguez

Production Editor: Melanie Birdsall

Copy Editor: Christobel Colleen Hopman

Typesetter: TNQ Technologies

Proofreader: Benny Willy Stephen

Cover Designer: Gail Buschman

Marketing Manager: Deena Meyer

Printed in Canada

ISBN 978-1-0718-0304-2

This book is printed on acid-free paper.

20 21 22 23 24 10 9 8 7 6 5 4 3 2 1

Contents

What constitutes positive reinforcement? It's not a matter of smothering children with praise. Positive reinforcement doesn't mean rewarding children with pizza and prizes. Nor does it involve hovering over them while they do worksheets, or drilling them on letters and words. Positive reinforcement simply means *focusing* on them, whether you're talking to them, listening to them, or singing or reading to them. What could make a child feel more loved than getting your undivided attention? What better way to help a child thrive?

There's no doubt that veteran early childhood professionals are seeing more challenging behavior in their settings these days. New teachers struggle as well with the amount of time spent handling behavior challenges. But why is this happening? I believe much of it results from changes to early childhood education. From the emphasis on academics and accountability, and the attempt to accelerate child development. In this chapter, I offer seven reasons I see behind the increase in disruptive behavior.

One of the reasons there are more behavior challenges than in the past is that we more often ask children to do things for which they're not developmentally equipped, and the frustration is causing them to act out. But what if we respected and appreciated children for who and what they are? What if we took child development into consideration when we determined our expectations? I promise that life in the classroom would be considerably easier!

Our education system is not set up to support children who refuse to comply with attempts to control and change them. Given the right environment, these children might well become the artists, innovators, and leaders among us. But we'll never know the magnitude of the potential lost, as children with strong, independent characters are too often either drugged or dismissed.

If there were a list of things that young children aren't suited (developmentally ready) to do, at the top of that list would be *being still* and *being quiet*. Yet those are two of the top requirements, along with forming a line (something else they're not adept at), that we try to impose on young children during most transitions. We then ask them to move from one place to another, pretending to hold bubbles in their mouths so they'll be silent. The result is often resistance and chaos. But it doesn't have to be that way.

Part II. Teaching With the Body in Mind

When children fall out of their chairs in classrooms on a regular basis (one teacher counted her first-graders doing so *44 times* in one week), we need to take a closer look at what's going on and at how our decisions and policies are impacting the course of human development.

When we advocate for kids to have more movement, we often encounter resistance due to the mistaken notion that children, just by virtue of being children, are constantly in motion. But nothing could be further from the truth, especially in many school and early childhood settings. A continuing stream of research proves it. But is anybody paying attention?

When you think of children in motion, do you imagine them bouncing off the walls? Fear of losing control of the children is one of the reasons teachers are sometimes disinclined to encourage movement in their settings. And, yes, movement can generate a lot of energy. But you might be surprised to learn that *lack* of movement is far more likely to create challenging behavior in your setting!

A study involving parents and teachers in 15 countries found that the majority believe the development of motor skills is important for their children. However, they evidently also assume motor skill development happens without adult intervention—because neither the parents nor the teachers felt it was their responsibility to promote it. Nor did they feel it was the responsibility of the other group. Unfortunately, that's an easy assumption to make—but it's neither correct nor helpful to children.

administrators for doing activities that once were considered developmentally appropriate. But we can't let uninformed policies take precedence over children's needs. So, if you're a teacher who has to or wants to sneak movement into the curriculum, this chapter is for you.

Part III. Teaching With Children's Futures in Mind

Part IV. Advocacy

When administrators ban such activities as cartwheels from school grounds—not because there have been any incidents, but because there *could* be one—they are not protecting the children. Rather, they're protecting themselves—from worry, from effort, and from the possibility of a lawsuit—putting their needs ahead of the children's.

In our fear-entrenched society, adults too often believe in fears of an imaginary nature, such as stranger danger, which even the Center for Missing and Exploited Children maintains is a myth. But such *truly* harmful issues as children's sedentary behavior, screen use, and lack of downtime are ignored.

I do understand that school safety drills have become a necessity. They are intended to keep kids and teachers safe, and in this case, preparing for potential harm makes sense. But, as with all decisions concerning children, shouldn't we keep the *children* in mind? Shouldn't school safety drills take into consideration the children's developmental levels and weigh the consequences of frightening them to the point of traumatizing them?

Do you know the story of Sisyphus? In Greek mythology, this former king of Corinth was punished in Hades by continually having to roll a huge boulder up a hill only to have it roll back down as soon as he got it to the summit. I'm sure many of us have felt that way at certain times in our lives, but perhaps no one feels it more than the person advocating for children—especially if that advocacy involves play.

Acknowledgments

T hanks to everyone at Corwin for helping to make this book
happen—especially Mia Rodriguez and Lucas Schleicher.
I'm particularly grateful to my editor, Jessica Allan, for her
enthusiastic response to my proposal and to the manuscript, and
to production editor Melanie Birdsall, for her heartfelt appreciation of my work! That kind of support is balm to a writer's soul!

As always, I need to give thanks for the friends who nurture
me: Sheila Chapman, Kelly O'Meara, Jody Martin, Jane Fitz-
patrick, Cecie Boggs, Gail Multop, Rebecca Isbell, and Nicole
Parent among them. I have an overabundance of riches when it
comes to the friendships and love in my life. Also, much gratitude
to two brilliant women who have offered me invaluable business
advice: April Wier and Maggie Ashley.

Finally, my deepest appreciation to the many early childhood
educators and parents who have attended my presentations, in
person and online, shared their stories with me, and who fight for
the right of children to be children!

Publisher's Acknowledgments

Corwin gratefully acknowledges the contributions of the
following reviewers:

Cynthia C. Massey
Assistant Professor
Georgia Southern University
Statesboro, GA

Christine Ruder
Teacher
Truman Elementary School
Rolla, MO

About the Author

Rae Pica has been an education consultant (www.raepica.com) specializing in the education and development of the whole child since 1980. A former adjunct instructor with the University of New Hampshire, she is the author of 21 books, including the text *Experiences in Movement and Music,* in its fifth edition, and *What If Everybody Understood Child Development?: Straight Talk About Bettering Education and Children's Lives.* Rae is known for her lively and informative keynotes and trainings, both virtual and live, and has shared her expertise with such groups as the *Sesame Street* Research Department, the Head Start Bureau, Centers for Disease Control, the President's Council on Physical Fitness and Sports, Nickelodeon's *Blue's Clues*, Gymboree, Nike, and state health departments throughout the country. Rae is a regular blogger and YouTube creator and the author of online courses for early childhood professionals.

Introduction

I once heard a workshop leader say, "We often set up environments for children that are contrary to what we know about who and what they are." I wish I could give credit to this obviously intelligent woman but, unfortunately, I don't remember who it was.

She was right of course. Moreover, we often *teach* in ways that are contrary to what we know about who and what children are. That's certainly true for today's young children and our unrealistic expectations of them—our propensity to hurry them beyond their developmental stage. It's true when considering our demand that they sit still to learn, our conviction that movement equals misbehavior, and our use of discipline practices, such as withholding recess or tracking behavior on charts, that go against what the research tells us.

Some of our actions are the result of the society in which we currently reside. For example, the belief that "earlier is better" has run rampant throughout this country and elsewhere. Some actions are the result of terrible education policies created by people who don't understand education or child development—and sometimes seem to not even like children. Some are taught in universities and depend on which theories and textbooks professors have adopted—theories that may very well contradict those of other professors and textbooks. And some of it comes down to one of my least favorite phrases in the English language: "It's always been done this way." That's certainly true of the sitting-to-learn concept, which is also a result of the long-held belief that the head and body have nothing to do with one another.

I recently came across an article titled "The ADHD Overdiagnosis Epidemic Is a Schooling Problem, Not a Child One." It opened with the following words:

Childhood exuberance is now a liability. Behaviors that were once accepted as normal, even if mildly irritating to adults, are increasingly viewed as unacceptable and cause for medical intervention. High energy, lack of impulse control, inability to sit still and listen, lack of organizational skills, fidgeting, talking incessantly—these typical childhood qualities were widely tolerated until relatively recently.

The piece went on to say that because these typical childhood characteristics are no longer widely tolerated, ADHD is being diagnosed at an astonishing rate, particularly among young children. Brain-altering drugs are often seen as the solution to the "problem."

But when did childhood become a problem? An ailment? Why can't we value it for the special, unique period that it is? Why can't we get schools ready for children, instead of requiring children to get ready for school? Why can't we teach children the way they learn, rather than treating them as empty vessels in need of filling? Young children are born with the desire to learn! Exploration and discovery are meant to define their early lives. When our school system refuses to acknowledge this and instead forces them to "learn" material that's developmentally or age inappropriate—and in ways they don't naturally learn—the desire to acquire knowledge withers and dies.

There's another consequence as well. As I write in Chapter 2, challenging behavior is on the increase—in a big way. Veteran teachers tell me they have never witnessed the kind of defiance and aggression that's now taking place in their classrooms. New teachers are both stunned and unprepared for the amount of time they spend coping with behavior issues. But I ask you: If you were forced to sit still for hours at a time, denied recreation and downtime, and your very personhood disrespected, wouldn't you also become defiant? I know I would.

I realize this book is not going to change overnight an education system that has been in place for almost 200 years. But I hope it will provoke readers to consider the number of other changes we've witnessed over the last two centuries, and why schooling isn't among them, except in the most negative of ways. To wonder why, instead of making use of all the incredible research we now possess—on child development, on the human brain, on how children learn best—decision-makers simply ignore it in favor of their own misguided priorities. To wonder why so many things are getting worse instead of better. And it certainly is getting worse for young children, who are currently expected to do that for which, developmentally speaking, they should not be expected to do. Whose health and happiness are being threatened by the erroneous notions circulating throughout our society, many of which I took on in my earlier book, *What If Everybody Understood Child Development?*

I don't believe that natural childhood behaviors should be pathologized. Nor do I believe they should be merely "tolerated." Rather, I wish we would *celebrate* all that childhood involves. It comes only once in a lifetime, and for such a brief period. Its joy and exuberance help us welcome the rest of our lives and to find our passions. It shapes the adults we become. If misinformed notions about education cause children to become profoundly unhappy (as the number of depressed and anxious children tells me they are), what kind of future lies ahead for them?

But what if we taught the way children learn? What if we honored their natural inclinations and *used* them, rather than fighting against them? What if we accepted that children don't exist only from the neck up and we valued their bodies as well as their brains? What if we better understood what would be most helpful for them in the future?

I believe we'd have far less challenging behavior. I believe our children would experience childhood as a joyful, discovery-filled time, as it's meant to be—and that their futures would be that much richer for it. I also believe they'd learn a lot more—certainly a lot more of what matters.

As was the case with *What If Everybody Understood Child Development?*, this book consists of short essays that run approximately 900–1,300 words in length, better meeting the needs of today's busy readers. You can easily and quickly read the pieces here whenever time allows, in whatever order preferred. There are 31 essays, divided among four categories: "Teaching With Children's Nature in Mind," "Teaching With the Body in Mind," "Teaching With Children's Futures in Mind," and "Advocacy." The latter section is offered for those of you who wish to fight for better education policies, and for the right of children to be children.

The opinions expressed in *What If We Taught the Way Children Learn?* are based on my four decades in the field, first as an educator and then as an educational consultant. But they're also supported by research, anecdotal evidence, stories shared by teachers and parents, and the views of experts in the fields of education, child development, play research, the neurosciences, and more. It's unlikely you'll agree with all of them. But whether or not you agree, it's my hope that the straight talk in this book will inspire and motivate you to generate change—so children can begin to have the lives and education they deserve.

PART I

Teaching With Children's Nature in Mind

CHAPTER 1

Giving Children the Positive Reinforcement They Want and Need

How many of these scenarios are familiar to you?

- A child creates something, and an adult rattles off a quick "Good job!" without really acknowledging the child's work.
- Children at home or in an early childhood setting are staring at screens rather than engaging with other children or with an adult.
- Infants, toddlers, and preschoolers are being taught to read instead of being read to.

These situations are the result of false beliefs running rampant throughout our society. The first is the result of the belief that we have to give children "positive reinforcement" in the way of praise in order to boost their self-esteem. The second stems from the twin beliefs that technology offers today's children the best learning opportunities, and that children must become acquainted with technology as early as possible, since it's going to be a part of their lives. And the last relates to the ubiquitous idea that the earlier children acquire skills like reading, the smarter and more successful they'll be.

Sadly, none of these myths result in children getting what they truly want and need.

I contend that no matter what myths may be circulating, we only have to hold one belief in our hearts: what children really want and need is the loving attention of the important adults in their lives. And I contend that if we focus on that one belief, parenting and early childhood education will be a lot simpler, and everybody (especially the children) will be a lot happier.

But what constitutes loving attention? It's not a matter of smothering children with praise and what most consider "positive reinforcement." Loving attention doesn't involve hovering over children while they do worksheets or sit at computers. It doesn't mean drilling them on letters and words. Rather, it simply means *focusing* on them, whether you're talking to them, listening to them, or singing or reading to them. What could make a child feel more special than being the recipient of your undivided attention? What better way is there to help a child thrive?

When I was growing up, my father was ill and in and out of hospitals, and my mom worked outside of the home, which was unusual in those days. Those two factors meant we had less time together and fewer outings than my friends' families had. It also means I have fewer memories of family time. But the one thing I remember very clearly is that we had dinner together every night my father was home—and I took advantage of the occasion to relay every detail about my day. I also recall that I felt listened to—because I was. And that experience has had a considerable and positive impact on me.

I thought about this when I watched Diane Sawyer's special about screen time. One little boy was talking to his mom while she looked at her phone. And when he took her face in his hands and asked her to listen to him with her "whole face," my heart could hardly stand it. All he wanted was her undivided attention. And, really, it wasn't asking a lot.

I thought of it again when a colleague wrote a blog post describing a scenario in which the teachers in an early childhood setting played one video after another for the children, rising from their seats only when it was time to change videos. Moreover, at lunchtime, the children watched a tablet positioned on their table, while the teachers ate by themselves at another table.

Yes, it may be challenging to provide undivided attention in an early childhood setting or classroom, where there's a room full of children. Still, when a teacher takes a moment to get down to the child's level while talking or listening to him or her, the child feels heard. When a teacher is reading to the children and making eye contact with each and every one of them, the children feel as though they matter. When an adult pauses to talk to the children about their work (which, according to psychology professor Ellen Ava Sigler, is the true definition of positive reinforcement), the children feel significant in a way that false praise or watching a screen could never make them feel.

Children really aren't complicated. All they want and need is you.

What's a Teacher to Do?

• When a child is communicating with you, don't forget to listen with your "whole face." Reggio Emilia teachers employ a "pedagogy of listening" because listening demonstrates respect and interest. This is all any of us really want from communication.

• Remember that words aren't always necessary when communicating with young children. You don't need to say "Good job!" when your eyes and your smile can do it for you. According to research, 70 percent of communication is nonverbal.

• Get down to the child's level so it's possible to look her or him in the eyes.

• Include touch, such as a high-five, a fist bump, or a hand on a shoulder or the back, whenever possible.

• Be sure to use the children's names often. We all love the sound of our names and feel special when we hear them spoken.

Where to Learn More

- Part 1 of Diane Sawyer's special can be found here:

  https://www.youtube.com/watch?v=GqeOWatgN9w
  &list=PLQOa26lW-uI-pNs2w7ie09BET5LY_xDOF

- Listen to the podcast "Creating Praise Junkies: Are You Giving Too Much 'Positive Reinforcement?'" Ellen Ava Sigler is a guest. It can be accessed here:

  https://www.bamradionetwork.com/track/creating-praise-junkies-are-you-giving-children-too-much-positive-reinforcement/

- You can access a paper titled "From Positive Reinforcement to Positive Behaviors: An Everyday Guide for the Practitioner," written by Ellen Ava Sigler and Shirley Aamidor, here:

  https://link.springer.com/article/10.1007%2Fs10643-004-0753-9. The paper appeared in *Early Childhood Education Journal*.

- In this minute-and-a-half video, a dad carries on a conversation with his baby boy, who can't even speak yet:

  https://www.youtube.com/watch?v=AY35eXTKVLY

  The video made the rounds on Facebook and was enormously popular among early childhood professionals. I suspect the reason it went viral is because it's so cute. But I was also struck by the good fortune of the baby involved. Not only is he learning a great deal about quality communication; also, getting so much of his dad's attention has to make him feel pretty darn special.

CHAPTER 2

Seven Reasons We're Seeing More Challenging Behavior in Early Childhood Settings

In four decades of working in the early childhood field, I have never heard so many professionals talk about the behavior challenges they're facing. Veteran teachers say they've never before seen so many children acting out—or with such intensity. And new teachers find they're quite unprepared to handle the challenging behavior they're experiencing. Both groups are frustrated by the amount of time wasted on classroom management.

Why is challenging behavior more of an issue these days? I imagine much of it results from the changes to early childhood education that have occurred over the past couple of decades—specifically, from the emphasis on academics and accountability, and the attempt to accelerate child development. These wrongheaded "reforms," I believe, are behind the seven situations I cite below, all resulting in the increase in disruptive behavior.

Children have almost no time to play. Early childhood researcher and professor Nancy Carlsson-Paige calls play "nature's plan" and "a biological drive." And experts all around the globe agree with her.

Not only is play part of nature's plan for human youngsters; also, it's part of the plan for the young of almost all creatures. Can you imagine if we insisted that kittens, puppies, and baby goats stay still? If we prevented them from frolicking and playing? The idea is ludicrous—and it should be just as ludicrous when we're discussing children. Yet today's children are prevented from playing in early childhood settings because too many policymakers and administrators believe they should spend their time more "productively." The tools that formerly fostered children's play—dramatic-play centers, costumes, blocks, and such—have been removed from most early childhood settings because they're seen as frivolous. And recess is eliminated in favor of more "instructional time."

So, when do today's children, who are also overscheduled in their so-called free time, have the chance to do what nature intended?

We are demanding that children accomplish things for which they are in no way developmentally equipped. We insist that three-year-olds sit still, learn to grasp a pencil properly, and memorize the meaning of words like *hypothesis* (words which, by the way, have absolutely no relevance in their lives) because they have to "get ready to be four." We ask four-year-olds to draw a picture of their family and write a sentence about it. We expect children to read by the end of kindergarten, ready or not. We require pre-schoolers to do the work of kindergartners, and kindergartners to do the work of first-graders, and so on up the line.

All of this puts enormous pressure on young children because they're so anxious to please the adults in their lives. When they continually are unable to comply with adult demands—because the natural course of child development doesn't allow them to—they become frustrated and unhappy.

Frustrated, unhappy children act out.

Children get little to no downtime. Remember lying on the ground and finding creatures in the clouds? Being released from school and having the rest of the day to play, read, or simply daydream? Seemingly endless summers during which you were free to do whatever you chose?

How many children do you know who have those options today?

Downtime is essential for everyone's mental health, *including* children. How are the little ones supposed to enjoy their lives when every moment is scheduled for them? When they have no time for free play (child-chosen and child-directed)? When they have no time to recharge?

How can we expect good behavior from children who are exhausted and stressed?

We treat children as though they exist only from the neck up and only their brains matter, when the research shows and good sense validates the importance of the mind–body connection. The failure to acknowledge this connection is the primary reason why play and movement are eliminated from early childhood classrooms—and why young children are forced to sit for long periods. And what sense does that make when research has also demonstrated that sitting increases fatigue and reduces concentration?

What does make sense is that tired children who are unable to concentrate will have a tendency to act out!

We stifle children's natural creativity and inherent love of learning through worksheets, standardized tests and curricula, and an insistence on conformity and rote—as opposed to active, authentic—learning. Children are born with a love of learning and are naturally creative, experiential learners. They're not meant to be empty vessels to be filled with useless information. This bores them, and a bored child is more likely to become restless and disruptive.

We pit children against one another with our focus on competition and winning. Competition is not developmentally appropriate for young children, who actually prefer *cooperative* activities to competitive ones. When children are more well-versed in competition than cooperation, the atmosphere in an early childhood setting is not as friendly as it should be. After all, as experts such as Alfie Kohn have informed us, competition increases aggression and other antisocial behaviors.

Too many children spend hours in front of screens, leading sedentary lives (the sitting thing again) filled with virtual relationships instead of interacting with real people in real life—when the research clearly shows that social–emotional development is critical in early childhood and *in-person interactions* are necessary for social–emotional development. Additionally, research has determined that screen time is creating depression and aggression in children.

With all of this, it's no wonder there are more challenging behaviors in early childhood settings. That children are acting out. How could all of these circumstances *not* lead to defiance? Defiance is often the only way young children are able to push back, as they don't have the cognitive ability to know what it is they're feeling or the verbal ability to express their feelings in words. So, what's left for them to do?

Heck, if all of this were being imposed on me, even at my age, I would probably act out, too!

What's a Teacher to Do?

• Determine not to see movement as misbehavior! Understand that the human body was meant to move, not sit, and that young children, more than any other members of the population, need to move in order to live and learn.

• If we can look at things through a child's eyes, we're more likely to avoid challenging behavior before it begins. For example, why would we expect young ones to stand still in a line and be quiet for transitions, when they're not yet developmentally capable of doing either of those things? Instead, if you stand at the head of the line and play a quiet game of Follow the Leader, transitions will be fun, engaging, and peaceful!

• You may no longer be allowed to include naptime as part of the day, but you should ensure that the children get *some* time to rest. Also, when possible, allow the children a bit of unstructured time during which they can choose what they'd like to do.

- Do away with competitive practices, such as gold stars and behavior charts, in your classroom. Instead, help the children learn to cooperate and collaborate with the learning activities and games you use.

- Limit—or, if possible, eliminate—screen time in your classroom, opting instead for active, authentic learning experiences.

Where to Learn More

- Nancy Carlsson-Paige discusses children's current inability to play in this 11-minute podcast:

  https://www.bamradionetwork.com/track/have-children-lost-their-ability-to-play/

- The American Academy of Pediatrics offers "The Importance of Play in Healthy Child Development and Maintaining Strong Parent-Child Bonds":

  https://pediatrics.aappublications.org/content/119/1/182

- Here's information about the study, conducted by University of Virginia researchers, demonstrating that kindergarten has become the new first grade:

  http://www.aera.net/Newsroom/News-Releases-and-Statements/Study-Snapshot-Is-Kindergarten-the-New-First-Grade

- Read "Why Your Brain Needs More Downtime":

  https://www.scientificamerican.com/article/mental-downtime/

- Read "'Schools Are Killing Curiosity': Why We Need to Stop Telling Children to Shut Up and Learn":

  https://www.theguardian.com/education/2020/jan/28/schools-killing-curiosity-learn

(Continued)

(Continued)

- To learn more about the role of the body in learning, you might read Eric Jensen's *Learning With the Body in Mind* or John Ratey's *Spark: The Revolutionary New Science of Exercise and the Brain*.

- Alfie Kohn's *No Contest: The Case Against Competition* is probably the quintessential book on the topic of competition.

- See "Two Hours Screen Time Linked to Children's Behavior Problems":

  https://www.techtimes.com/articles/241842/20190419/ two-hours-screen-time-linked-to-childrens-behavioral- problems.htm

- Read "The Scary, Lasting Effects of Too Much Screen Time on Children":

  https://www.marketwatch.com/story/the-scary-lasting- effects-of-too-much-screen-time-on-children-2019-04-10

- *Acting Out!: Avoid Behavior Challenges With Active Learning Games & Activities* offers research and advice on the topic of challenging behavior, along with 200 activities that promote community building, prosocial skills, self-regulation, and relaxation.

CHAPTER 3

Commonsense Solutions to Behavior Challenges

I recently wrote a book about avoiding behavior challenges, and as I was writing, it occurred to me that so many challenges can be prevented if we (1) appreciate and respect childhood for what it is and (2) employ common sense!

Or, perhaps those two go together. Common sense should tell us that children are not small adults and can't be expected to act like anything other than what they are: children. Still, in many early childhood programs, children are expected to be able to sit for endless minutes and hours, stay still, be quiet, and stand in straight lines—despite the fact that they're not yet developmentally ready to do any of those things. And when young children display their inability to do these things, they're thought to be misbehaving.

Yes, I know they will eventually have to be able to do everything mentioned above. But eventually most will also need to learn to drive a car. That doesn't mean we should put them behind the wheel while they're still preschoolers.

As I wrote in the last chapter, I'm convinced one of the reasons we're seeing more behavior challenges than in the past is that we're more often asking children to do things for which they're not equipped, and the frustration is causing them to act out. I mean, if someone insisted over and over again that I fly a plane or perform surgery, for instance, I'd get pretty frustrated too!

One of the things common sense tells us is that young children need to *move*! But many teachers hesitate to make movement and active learning part of their programs because when they think of children and movement, they immediately form a mental image of children "bouncing off the walls." The concept of *movement* as an approach to avoiding behavior challenges feels like an oxymoron. But the truth is, children allowed to move as often as possible are far *less* likely to wreak havoc upon the classroom.

And it's important to note that regardless of how active the children are, if we employ common sense, we can still have a peaceful environment. For example, we've all been taught to begin where the children are, developmentally speaking. If we start from where they are and build from there with a logical progression of skills, we'll ensure the children are challenged but not overwhelmed. Not only can we expect greater success from children asked merely to build on their earlier successes; also, we can expect them to act out less often.

Similarly, you'll have fewer behavior challenges if you use your voice as a tool. If you want the children to move slowly, speak slowly. If you want them to move quietly, speak quietly. In addition, just as you can catch more flies with honey than with vinegar, you can attract more attention with a lower volume than with a higher one, as children are far more likely to react positively to a whisper than to a yell.

Remember, too, although you should present your challenges enthusiastically, if you maintain a fever pitch of enthusiasm, the children will become overstimulated. I witnessed this once when working as a university adjunct. One of my students was conducting a lesson with a group of five-year-olds and spoke to them at an extremely high-pitched, rapid pace throughout. By the time she asked them to move like turtles, what she got was a group of *racing* turtles!

Certainly, there are times when kids just being kids can make you feel as though you've lost control of them. But if you *expect* children to act like children (and their acting like children is okay with you), you can get ahead of potential issues and nip them in the bud. Following are three typical situations we've all experienced, along with solutions:

- You hand out equipment or props to the children and expect them to stand silently, holding onto them and awaiting your instructions with bated breath. But how realistic is that? Young children are playful and inquisitive! If you simply allow them a few moments to experiment with the props and get it out of their system, they're much more likely to be ready and willing to listen to you and follow your directions.
- You've asked the children to gather around but some just aren't interested, perhaps because they're in the middle of something they consider more important. It you get started with those who are interested, others will eventually join in—because young children are curious and don't want to feel left out.
- In the same way, if you've asked the children to group themselves by twos for a game or activity and there are those who object to the child they're paired with, start without them! There's no reason to spend time debating with them—and taking time away from the children who are ready to go—when ignoring their behavior is so much more effective. If you begin without them, chances are very good that they'll partner up and join in.

Speaking of taking partners: if you make a game out of it, you'll have a greater success rate. With an activity called Back to Back, you ask the children to get back to back with someone else as quickly and quietly as they can. You then count down, dramatically, from five to zero, at which point the children should all be paired up. Typically, the children will be more concerned with how quickly they can get back to back than with whom they're pairing up—because they love games and they love a challenge. But if one of the children complains about his or her partner, implement the practice above.

There will be times, of course, when you wonder if there isn't an easier way to make a living. (I know I did!) These suggestions may not guarantee you'll never again be tempted to look for a less challenging occupation, but I can guarantee they'll help avoid behavior challenges and create a positive learning environment.

What's a Teacher to Do?

• Remind yourself that you went into early childhood education because you love children—and children are supposed to act like children!

• Remember that there is a process involved, created by nature, allowing children to eventually be able to sit and stand still. Among other things, nature's plan involves movement, which helps develop the proprioceptive and vestibular senses required for sitting and standing still.

• Remind yourself that *intrinsic* motivation is what we're after when we teach children. Punishment and rewards are all about extrinsic motivation. Young children are intrinsically motivated by that which feels good—that which is fun—and a game like Back to Back is fun. The same is true of Follow the Leader, used for transitions, as mentioned in the last chapter.

• If you consider movement misbehavior, reflect on why that might be. Remind yourself that the human body was designed to move, not sit.

• Remember—really remember—the joy of movement you experienced as a child.

Where to Learn More

- For information on how a lack of movement is impacting the development of the proprioceptive and vestibular systems, read "The Shocking Phenomenon That Shows Just How Movement-Starved Modern Kids Really Are":

  https://www.stack.com/a/the-shocking-phenomenon-that-shows-just-how-movement-starved-modern-kids-really-are

- Angela Hansom's book *Balanced and Barefoot* does an excellent job helping us understand why children can't sit still, pay attention, and so forth. Angela is a pediatric occupational therapist and knows what she's talking about.

- For straight talk about bettering children's lives and education—and better understanding young children—read *What If Everybody Understood Child Development?*, published by Corwin.

- I've created a two-hour online course titled "Avoid Challenging Behavior in Your Early Childhood Setting." You can find it here:

  https://raepica.teachable.com/p/avoid-challenging-behavior-in-early-childhood-settings

CHAPTER 4

Disruptive Children: Are Drugging and Dismissing Them Our Only Options?

In this educational era, resonating with appeals for standards and standardization, driven by the requirements of accountability and evaluation, the words, metaphors, and images that come to our minds and haunt our public consciousness carry just the opposite meaning: they speak of uniformity and conformity, management and control, of achievement and success as measured by narrow assessment tools and remote, quantifiable metrics. They tend to be blind to, and mute about, those powerful dimensions of classroom life that are shaped through intimate relationships, through community building, through honoring the rich variations and differences among us.

They do not recognize or appreciate that education is a complex human enterprise requiring creativity and imagination, heart, mind, and soul, struggle and suffering, grit and grace. In our efforts to control and measure, in fact, we often confuse difference with deviance, illness with identity; we pathologize, exclude, and then label those children who do not fit the norm—who trouble the waters, who misbehave—and we reward the teachers who contain and squelch the troublemakers.

These words are from the foreword, written by Sara Lawrence-Lightfoot, to a heartbreaking book called *Troublemakers: Lessons in Freedom From Young Children at School*, by Carla Shalaby. The book is painful to read, but I believe it's important that every educator tackle it.

Shalaby, an educator herself, tells the story of 4 six- and seven-year-old students, whom she observed both in school and at home. She chose these four children by asking teachers to identify the students who presented the most challenging behaviors in their classrooms. They are among the students whom she's witnessed, in her many classroom visits, being regularly punished—"reprimanded, detained, isolated, removed." She adds:

They are not described as leaders, as children from whom we might learn. Instead, the descriptions are invariably disparaging: angry, damaged, disturbed, out of control, impossible. Justifications for their daily mistreatment are made on the basis of their own alleged bad behavior, as if they themselves have chosen to be treated as less than fully human in school.

Shalaby refers to these children as miners' canaries—because she sees their disruptions as "a signal cry…that there is poison in our shared air." It is a disturbing and painful comparison but, I'm afraid, an accurate one. Shalaby points to the "toxic social and cultural conditions of schools" and hopes that by shedding light on the stories of these "troublemakers," educators and parents will look to clean the air, rather than force children to tolerate the poison.

I must say that the teachers of the four children profiled in this book were good teachers in many ways. But even they failed these children—in large part because our education system is not set up to support children who refuse to comply with attempts to control and change them. Given the right environment, they might well become the artists, innovators, and leaders among us. We'll never know the magnitude of the potential lost, as children with strong, independent characters are too often either drugged or dismissed.

Troublemakers brings to mind two sayings that periodically make the rounds on social media, the first of which is the inspiration for the title of this book: *If kids aren't learning the way we teach, maybe we should teach the way they learn.* And: *Instead of preparing kids for school we should be preparing schools for kids.*

Why, I wonder, should these be novel ideas? Why are we putting *systems* and *institutions* above the needs of our children? We proclaim that we value children above all else, but I see too little evidence of that in the decisions that have been made, and continue to be made, on their "behalf."

Why, I wonder, are we more eager to drug and/or dismiss children than to honor and respect them?

What's a Teacher to Do?

• Do everything in your power not to take the children's behavior personally.

• When a child acts out, pause to ask yourself if the child is truly misbehaving or is simply engaging in childlike behavior.

• When a child acts out, stop and recall the words of Dr. Jody Carrington, who wrote, "Every time you think of calling a kid 'attention-seeking,' consider changing it to 'connection-seeking' and see how your perspective changes."

• Communicate with the parents and families of the children in your care. Lack of communication with and empathy for parents has been cited as a prime reason behind expulsions.

• Use some of the methods described in the last section of this book—and whatever others you can—to fight back against a system that punishes children and rewards teachers for doing so.

Where to Learn More

- Walter Gilliam is the ultimate expert on the subject of preschool expulsions. This nine-minute video featuring Dr. Gilliam provides a brief overview of who's being expelled and why:

  https://www.youtube.com/watch?v=EQqAQgBwJxY

- Watch Rosemarie Allen's TEDx Talk, "School Suspensions Are an Adult Behavior":

  https://www.youtube.com/watch?v=f8nkcRMZKV4

  Dr. Allen tells her audience that from the time she entered school, she was suspended at least seven times a year!

- It behooves all of us to reflect on our potential biases. In this 11-minute podcast, Rosemarie Allen and educator Jason Flom discuss the question, "Do You Treat Black and White Students Differently?":

  https://www.bamradionetwork.com/track/do-you-treat-black-and-white-students-differently/

- This article provides an overview of a study showing a correlation between stronger connections with parents and reduced preschool expulsions:

  https://www.educationdive.com/news/study-to-reduce-preschool-expulsions-form-stronger-connections-with-paren/551763/

- An article in *The Wall Street Journal*, although an opinion piece, offers information regarding studies on the topic. Titled "We're Overmedicating Our Children," it can be found here:

  https://www.wsj.com/articles/were-overmedicating-our-children-11551917025

CHAPTER 5

Trouble-Free Transitions: They're Possible If We Understand Child Development

I f there were a list of things that young children aren't suited (developmentally ready) to do, the top of that list would include *being still* and *being quiet*. Yet those are the exact two requirements we try to impose on young children during most transitions. We insist that they form an orderly line, stand still, and refrain from talking, all of which they're also not adept at.

We then ask them to move from one place to another in that manner, pretending to hold bubbles in their mouths so they'll be silent.

If we truly understand child development, why are we asking children to do that which they're not yet equipped to do? Are we showing respect for who and what young children are when we ask them to hold those bubbles in their mouths? Or is this simply a desire for control?

Don't get me wrong; I'm not a fan of chaos. I absolutely want the children to do as I ask! But if I'm asking them to do what they're not yet capable of doing—and for which they have no intrinsic motivation—resistance and chaos are what I can expect. Young children *perceive* when we're disrespecting them, and they make us pay for that.

The end result is exasperation, and even anger, on the part of both the children and the teachers. And that isn't pretty. During site visits I've witnessed teachers who resorted to yelling at the kids to get them to comply. So, it's no wonder transitions come to be dreaded by everyone involved. And it's no wonder that many experts refer to transitions as a waste of learning time. How can learning take place in such an environment?

But it doesn't have to be this way! Instead of fighting to get the kids to move quietly up a flight of stairs, why not challenge them to pretend to be climbing a mountain? Or, if that still results in too much noise (I happen to believe that *sound* is acceptable as long as it isn't interfering with others), the children can be invited to pretend they're weightless astronauts, or cats stalking a bird. Or how about a game of Follow the Leader, with the teacher at the head of the line, tiptoeing in exaggerated silence up the stairs? The children would love that!

Of course, in addition to eliminating chaos (children aren't inclined to wreak havoc when they're engaged), there are clearly learning opportunities here as well. With just a little imagination, transitions can be linked to themes and lessons being explored in the classroom, adding continuity and the repetition necessary for young children to "cement" the information acquired. Activities like these also offer chances for problem-solving, creativity, and self-expression—and we can't ever have too much of those. They're among the skills we can be *certain* kids will need in this rapidly changing world.

Because transitions usually require moving from one place to another—and music is a common partner of movement, as well as being mood altering—movement and music are the perfect tools for transitions, as well as being two subjects today's teachers have trouble finding ample time for. Children *love* movement and music, so that alone helps turn transitions into pleasurable experiences—even something to look forward to. Movement activities, songs (piggyback songs can be created for any occasion), and fingerplays provide a focus for the children during transitions, hold the attention of waiting kids, and are easily tied to curriculum.

For example, if you've been studying animals, you can invite the children to move like some of the quietest ones: foxes, turtles, or rabbits, to name a few. If you've been studying the weather, you can ask them to transition as though they're clouds, sunshine, or a gentle breeze.

Additionally, the children will learn to bring satisfactory closure to activities during successful transitioning, and they'll learn to move easily into and out of group situations. These dynamics naturally entail cooperation and consideration, which are important social–emotional skills. *And* the children will learn to follow directions—which is often the argument made for more "stringent" transitions.

If we truly understand child development, we know that young children have no motivation to learn something unless it's fun and engaging (that's where their intrinsic motivation comes from). If we make following directions fun and engaging, they'll learn to follow directions. And if we handle transitions in imaginative and developmentally appropriate ways—and *plan* them, as we plan other parts of the program—transitions will be both trouble-free and filled with significant learning experiences.

What's a Teacher to Do?

• Planning transitions doesn't mean you have to create lesson plans. But if you prepare for them as you prepare other parts of your day, you'll find transitions not just more tolerable but actually pleasurable!

• Make necessary preparations in advance, a suggestion that goes hand in hand with the one above. If you have a collection of fingerplays, piggyback songs, and activities on hand for every kind of transition, you won't have to search your brain for something at the last minute, and there'll be much less waiting involved for the children. Less waiting means less disruption.

(Continued)

(Continued)

• Remain calm and collected during transitions. If you appear unhinged, the children will become unhinged, too. But if you move slowly and speak softly, the children will respond in kind.

• If a transition involves taking turns—for example, when donning outerwear—ensure that the same children don't always go first. You might invite all the children wearing blue to first go to the coatroom one day and all the children with brown eyes the next day. Children will wait their turn if they understand that they will eventually get one.

Where to Learn More

• There are many ideas for transition activities, for different parts of the day, on my YouTube channel:

https://www.youtube.com/channel/UC-d20r_dzRuJd Q7J0TEZOMQ

• You'll find even more transition activities in my book, *Teachable Transitions: 190 Activities to Move From Morning Circle to the End of the Day.*

• "Make Transitions Trouble-Free & Teachable!" is an online course for early childhood professionals. It reviews the trouble with traditional transitions, explores how transitions can be linked to learning, and offers tips for making transitions chaos-free and fun, as well as numerous suggested transition activities:

https://raepica.teachable.com/p/make-transitions-trouble-free-teachable/

- Listen to the 11-minute podcast, "Creating Trouble-Free Transitions," involving four early childhood professionals:

  https://www.bamradionetwork.com/track/creating-trouble-free-transitions-2/

- *Young Children*, the journal of NAEYC, offers an article called "Reducing Challenging Behaviors During Transitions: Strategies for Early Childhood Educators to Share With Parents." You'll find it here:

  https://www.naeyc.org/resources/pubs/yc/sep2018/reducing-challenging-behaviors-during-transitions

CHAPTER 6

Fostering Self-Regulation: Are We Doing It Wrong?

Buzzwords and goals come and go in every field. In the early childhood field, *self-regulation* has been both a buzzword and a very big goal for children for a few years now. I suspect that's because, as I've written previously, challenging behaviors are on the rise in early childhood and school settings. The feeling is that if only every child could self-regulate, we'd see far fewer behavior issues!

The problem is, there is often confusion about what self-regulation is and how it should be fostered.

With regard to its definition, many believe it's all about self-control. And while self-control is indeed a part of it, self-regulation specifically refers to the ability to regulate *oneself* without intervention from an outside source, such as another person. In the case of young children, it means adults don't always have to be telling them how to behave; they've learned to control their emotions and resist impulsive behavior *on their own*.

Obviously, that's a good thing; the ability to regulate oneself is something we want for every individual. But, given its definition, many are going about "teaching" it in the wrong way: insisting that children *sit still* or *be quiet*, and assuming that once children are able to meet these unrealistic expectations, they will have acquired the ability to self-regulate. However, this fails to meet the primary characteristic of self-regulation: that there be no intervention from an outside source. Also, such demands are typically met with resistance—that is, challenging behavior—because, developmentally speaking, young children weren't created to sit still or stay quiet.

So, how *do* we go about promoting its development?

It's quite possible this might surprise you (or maybe not, if you know my work), but one of the best ways for children to learn to regulate themselves is through movement games! As with anything else, if it's *fun* for them, they're much more inclined to want to do it.

For example, if you ask children to stay still, it's not likely to happen. However, if you're playing a game of Statues, where they move while the music is playing and freeze into a statue when the music is paused, they'll *want* to stay still—because pretending to be a statue is fun!

Similarly, moving slowly requires a great deal more self-control than moving quickly.

Telling children to move slowly won't inspire them to learn how. But asking them to move like an astronaut floating in outer space—or as though they're trying to walk through peanut butter—provides incentive for them to move slowly. And, therefore, they learn how.

The same applies to the ability to wait. Waiting is definitely not a young child's strong suit. But if you give them a good reason to wait, they're more than happy to do it. What's a good reason to wait? How about an activity like Blast Off, where the children crouch low while you count backward from 10, with as much drama as possible? Not until you say "Blast off!" are the children to launch themselves.

Human development professor Lori Skibbe and her fellow researchers followed a group of children from preschool to second grade and used the game of Simon Says to determine the children's ability to self-regulate. They discovered that the earlier children acquired their self-regulation skills, the faster the skills developed. Their study also found that the benefits of self-regulation don't dwindle over time. Moreover, the study demonstrated that, beyond the improved behavior it offers, the ability to self-regulate also expands the young child's language and literacy development. Obviously, then, we have many good reasons to foster it.

If we know that young children aren't developmentally ready to be either still or quiet, why do we regularly ask them to do so and expect they'll comply? And if we know that joy is what inspires and motivates young children—and that movement is their preferred mode of learning—why aren't we more often taking advantage of this knowledge?

What's a Teacher to Do?

• When children don't comply with your request that they sit still or be quiet, understand that it's not usually defiance on their part. They're simply acting like children. Their lack of compliance more often indicates an inability, rather than an unwillingness, to do something.

• If children do obey your request to sit still or be quiet, don't praise them. This promotes the idea that compliance is what you value, and because your praise serves as extrinsic motivation, it won't benefit them in the long term.

• Remember that fostering intrinsic motivation is critical in the early years, and what motivates young children is that which is fun and feels good to them.

• Put together a collection of games, such as Statues and Blast Off, that you can rely on, as needed, and that promote true self-regulation. (There are resources listed on the following page that can help with this.)

• Share such children's books as *I Can Do That!* by Kayla Marnach and *I Can Handle It!* by Laurie Wright.

Where to Learn More

- Information about Skibbe's research can be found in "The Child's Ability to Self-Regulate Is a Critical Element in Childhood Language and Literacy Development":

  https://theeconomyofmeaning.com/2018/06/04/the-childs-ability-to-self-regulate-is-a-critical-element-in-childhood-language-and-literacy-development/

- Although intended primarily for parents (and misnamed), there's much good information in this podcast interview called "Teaching Children Self-Control," with psychology professor Laura Berk:

  https://www.bamradionetwork.com/track/teaching-children-self-control-2/

- *Acting Out!: Avoid Behavior Challenges With Active Learning Games & Activities* by Rae Pica includes a chapter of games that foster self-regulation.

- Videos with game suggestions are available on the YouTube channel *Active Learning With Rae*:

  https://www.youtube.com/channel/UC-d20r_dzRuJd Q7J0TEZOMQ

CHAPTER 7

Logical Consequences Should Be the Norm

Not long ago I had the unique experience of being interviewed by a middle school student. Jacob had found me on the Internet because he was researching recess and wanted to ask some questions for his project. Of course, recess is one of my favorite topics so I agreed to give him some time. What I didn't know until we were on the phone was the reason *behind* his project.

It seems he and a friend (a student with special needs) had had a small incident on the playground during the 10 minutes or so they got to hang out after lunch. As a result of the incident, not only had he and his friend had recess withheld, but so, too, had the *whole school*!

I was momentarily rendered speechless (a rare occurrence)— and I'm still angered when I think about it, even though I can imagine the theory behind this ludicrous decision. The principal—or whomever took the action—intended to *shame* these two kids into future good behavior. She or he was convinced that if the rest of the kids turned on these two, it would remind them to behave themselves going forward. His/her first mistake was in believing that you can cause children to do better by making them feel worse. Shaming—whether it's in the form of an action like this, putting a child in a corner, or those appalling behavior charts—is never the answer.

And where were the logical consequences? As explained by Responsive Classroom:

> *Logical consequences are respectful of the child's dignity while punishment often calls upon an element of shame. Logical consequences respond to the misbehavior in ways that preserve the dignity of the child. The message is that the behavior is a problem, not that the child is a problem.*

Even if shaming *was* effective—and, in this case, given how the adolescent brain works, it's highly doubtful—what is the rationale for punishing the rest of the kids? How could any administrator/decision-maker believe that's an appropriate reaction? That withholding recess for the whole school could be considered a teachable moment? Could it be that a logical consequence required too much effort to determine?

Of course, it's easy to believe that withholding recess *is* a logical consequence for misconduct on the playground. But let's think about that. Imagine that a couple of kids have a food fight in the cafeteria. A logical consequence would be making the kids clean up their mess and perhaps being made to clean all of the tables. That lets them know that nobody else is going to clean up after them. They also learn just how much work is involved in keeping a cafeteria clean—and, hopefully, some respect for the hardworking cafeteria employees, grudging though it may be, will also result. Withholding food for the rest of the week certainly wouldn't be an option! And detention, the most typical punishment, likely wouldn't have the hoped-for result: that the kids would use the time to consider the seriousness of their actions.

But in the playground example, what are the kids learning if the consequence is having recess withheld? Even if the child posed a risk to himself or someone else (and that's the only time a child should be *temporarily* removed from the playground), he's not learning responsibility if we simply force him to stay indoors. And he's certainly not learning behavior management or proper social interaction. He just becomes upset—and the longer he goes without recess, the antsier and more upset he'll get. Neither of those conditions is likely to improve behavior or teach appropriate social interaction.

I often use reading as an illustration: If a child is having trouble reading, we don't take away her books; we figure out what the problem is and then help her address it. Similarly, if a child is acting out in the classroom, we don't deny her an education. (I wrote about suspensions in *What If Everybody Understood Child Development?*) Nor should we take away recess if a child misbehaves on the playground.

In all cases of misbehavior, we should figure out what the problem is and then help the child address it. If a consequence is called for, it should be one that relates to the infraction and truly teaches the child a lesson worth learning.

Our children go to school to learn. Not just facts and figures, but how to become members of society. For that reason alone, a logical consequence should always be the norm, and the time it takes to conceive of one should be considered time well spent.

What's a Teacher to Do?

• The first task, if there's any confusion about the nature of logical consequences versus punishment, is to do a bit of research. The resources listed on the next page offer help along those lines.

• Take some time to reflect on your thoughts relative to punishment versus discipline. If necessary, remind yourself that you went into teaching because you love children, and that shaming is neither an expression of love nor respect.

• Given that there are behavior issues common to every classroom, you might want to make a list of them, along with appropriate consequences, in advance. That way you won't be left struggling to determine a logical consequence on the spur of the moment.

(Continued)

(Continued)

• When determining whether or not a true infraction has occurred and a logical consequence necessary, consider the student's culture. If, for example, you've asked the children to pair off for a partner activity and one child declines, it could be due to beliefs about personal space or appropriate touching. Or, perhaps you've used a simple gesture that you see as innocent but that the child sees as threatening.

Where to Learn More

• Responsive Classroom has an excellent article, "Punishment vs. Logical Consequences," at

https://www.responsiveclassroom.org/punishment-vs-logical-consequences/

• Education World offers a series of three helpful articles on logical consequences. The first is "Logical Consequences Teach Important Lessons":

https://www.educationworld.com/a_curr/columnists/charney/charney005.shtml

The second is "The Three R's of Logical Consequences":

https://www.educationworld.com/a_curr/columnists/charney/charney006.shtml

The final piece is "Examples of Logical Consequences":

https://www.educationworld.com/a_curr/columnists/charney/charney007.shtml

• You can listen to Dr. Muriel Rand, author of *The Positive Classroom* and *The Positive Preschool*, and educator/director Jason Flom discuss "Logical Consequences: Nuanced Responses to Student Misbehavior" here:

https://www.bamradionetwork.com/track/logical-consequences-nuanced-responses-to-student-behavior/

- An excellent source for understanding the role of culture in teaching is Zaretta Hammond's *Culturally Responsive Teaching and the Brain.*

CHAPTER 8

Screen Use in the Classroom: Why It's Cause for Concern

In the past, the early childhood classroom was a place where children discovered scientific principles at sand and water tables. Where they improved their fine motor skills with such activities as finger painting, molding play dough, and building with blocks. Where they improved their mathematical skills by sorting and stacking manipulatives. Where emergent literacy involved children curling up in the reading corner and happily perusing their favorite books. Where they donned cowboy hats, capes, and crowns in the dramatic-play area and acquired social–emotional skills that would serve them throughout life.

Today, it would be a happy surprise to witness such practices. Because today scenarios such as these are far too often believed to be old-fashioned and of little value. Today, far too many children, if not seated and hunched over worksheets, are seated in front of computers, laptops, or tablets, viewing videos or "learning" from apps.

Such scenes are being played out in preschools and kindergartens everywhere. And, in the early elementary years, computers are even more ubiquitous. The arrival of digital devices in classrooms is heralded and celebrated, much in the way art and music teachers used to be.

There are two prevailing beliefs that excite the public about the use of technology in the classroom and cause even the teachers of our youngest children to incorporate digital devices into their days. One is that technology is educational. How can finger painting compete with that? And the other belief is that, because technology will now be a large part of children's lives, we should get them acquainted with it as soon as possible.

But it appears little thought is given to the downsides of these beliefs. To what are, in fact, serious consequences—specifically to the notion of "as soon as possible."

Let's start with myopia, which is increasing at an alarming rate among children and is *directly* attributed to too much screen time and too little sunlight. Also known as nearsightedness, it might not at first seem like such a big deal. But in addition to causing blurred vision, which can impact academic and athletic performance, it is a progressive disease and can lead to such conditions as glaucoma, cataracts, and retinal detachment.

Another potential consequence related to vision is retinal damage. Digital devices emit a blue light that is more harmful to children than to adults. Children absorb more blue light than do adults because their lenses have yet to develop the pigmentation necessary to protect them. Not only does blue light suppress the production of melatonin, the hormone necessary for healthful sleep; also, because the light travels to the back of the eye, the macula can be damaged. The macula is the part of the retina with a high concentration of photoreceptor cells, which detect light and send signals to the brain, which in turn interprets the signals as images. The signs of macular degeneration, a disease that causes loss of central vision and was once seen primarily in aging individuals, are now observed in much younger people. My mother and aunt suffer from macular degeneration, so I've witnessed the anguish it can produce.

To me, the vision issues alone are cause for concern and caution. However, as they say on TV: But wait, there's more! Below is just a sampling.

- As I discuss in Chapter 15, today's young children can *swipe* (babies primarily accustomed to screens will even try to swipe books) but don't have the strength to tear a piece of paper. Here's where finger painting wins, hands down (pun intended).

- Lack of physical activity is an overwhelming problem. Not only do we have an obesity crisis (a term I hesitate to employ because its overuse now means people fail to take it seriously); also, we have children with severely undeveloped physical skills. And I'm not talking about the ability to throw a ball or run a race. I'm talking about children with so little core strength that they can't sit up straight. With so little physical strength in general that they're winded and exhausted after walking a block! These are stories that I hear over and over again from teachers.
- A 2017 study found that the more time a child spends with handheld screens, the more their expressive language is delayed.
- As I was writing this book, a new study determined that children ages three to five who use screens more than the recommended hour per day have lower levels of development in the brain's white matter. This is an area of the brain essential to development of language, literacy, and cognitive skills.

Adults (teachers, parents, administrators, policymakers) will argue that digital devices are a part of our society and the children's future. Well, let me paraphrase my friend Cindy Eckard, a woman on a mission to reduce screen use in classrooms: If we're allowing children's health to be destroyed, what kind of future do they have anyway?

What's a Teacher to Do?

- The most obvious recommendation is to reduce screen use as much as possible—and even *eliminate* it entirely in favor of hands-on, active learning.

- Get the children outside, where they'll be exposed to sunlight, as often as possible. Sunshine has been shown to mitigate the development of myopia.

(Continued)

(Continued)

• The research shows there's no benefit to homework in the elementary years, so abolishing it entirely isn't an unreasonable idea. But if for some reason you must assign it, determine not to give homework that requires a digital device.

• Teach children to recognize and report when their eyes are "tired."

• Alert parents to the health hazards of screen use. Endorse the value of outdoor play!

• Don't use laptops in place of computers. If the children have access to laptops only, make sure they're ergonomically correct through the use of monitor stands adjusted to the proper height and an exterior keyboard and mouse.

• Manufacturers of digital devices have created safety guidelines for the use of their products (although schools regularly fail to adhere to them). These guidelines include ergonomic considerations, recommendations for monitor height and angle, settings to reduce glare, and more. To protect your students' health, familiarize yourself with them.

• Cindy Eckard advises that you "review classroom seating and overhead lighting to minimize glare and reflection from windows or other light sources" and "require proper posture to avoid muscular discomfort."

Where to Learn More

- Cindy Eckard's website has an abundance of valuable advice. You'll find it here:

  http://www.screensandkids.us/

- Cindy joins Dr. Victoria Dunckley, author of *Reset Your Child's Brain*, and education leader Jill Berkowicz for a discussion about the impact of screen time on students here:

  https://www.bamradionetwork.com/track/do-you-know-enough-about-the-impact-of-screen-time-on-students/

- You can find information about blue light and vision here:

  https://www.reviewofoptometry.com/article/seeing-blue-the-impact-of-excessive-blue-light-exposure

- Here's information regarding a 2016 study demonstrating the increase in childhood myopia:

  https://news.usc.edu/91007/usc-eye-institute-study-seeks-cures-to-childhood-myopia/

- Read "Too Much Screen Time Linked to an Epidemic of Myopia Among Young People" here:

  https://medicalxpress.com/news/2019-02-screen-linked-epidemic-myopia-young.html

- Here's a CNN report about Dr. Catherine Birken's 2017 study concerning screen use and communication delays:

  https://www.cnn.com/2017/05/04/health/babies-screen-time-speech-delays-study/index.html

- "MRIs Show Screen Time Linked to Lower Brain Development in Preschoolers" can be found here:

  https://www.cnn.com/2019/11/04/health/screen-time-lower-brain-development-preschoolers-wellness/index.html

CHAPTER 9

Downtime: Necessary for Children's Mental Health and 21st Century Skills

Think back to your own childhood and the amount of downtime you had. Do you remember lying on your back outdoors, looking for creatures in the clouds? Being outside with friends and having the freedom to choose whatever game you wanted to play, or whatever drama you wanted to enact? Being alone in your bedroom, curled up on the bed and reading a beloved book, or quietly acting out a story with your dolls, action figures, or stuffed animals?

I remember all of those things. But, sadly, today's children won't have such memories because they aren't being granted the same opportunities for downtime. Instead, too many of today's children are leading overscheduled lives. Their lives are all about what they must *do*. There is no time for them just to *be*.

Intuitively, we know that everyone, including children, needs downtime. No one, even the most energetic among us, cares to rush through their waking hours, day after day after day. We know how stressful it is to be overscheduled, overpressured, and overwhelmed. We've witnessed the toll it takes on adults (on us!)—and it's horrible to imagine *children* feeling this way.

Despite this, many parents are afraid to let their children simply "do nothing." They worry that if they don't keep their children busy, busy, busy, they'll have résumés that look sparse in comparison to their counterparts. (Yes, we are now thinking in terms of résumés for our young children.)

Then, of course, we have policymakers like the Maryland school chief who declared it was time to do away with the "baby stuff," referring to naptime in preschool. Similar attitudes throughout the country have resulted in preschoolers and kindergartners being forced to *power through* their exhaustion in order to spend more time on "academics."

Unfortunately, such policies once again fail to consider the research. Dr. James Maas, an international authority on sleep and performance, has said that, among other things, being overtired leads to:

- Reduced ability to concentrate
- Reduced ability to remember
- Reduced ability to be creative
- Reduced ability to make critical decisions

None of that contributes to optimal performance in a classroom! Moreover, Dr. Mary Sheedy Kurcinka, author of *Sleepless in America*, contends that "a very significant percentage of challenging behaviors are actually the result of tired kids."

Yes, we want to help prepare our children for their future. But living an overscheduled, overprogrammed life isn't the way to do it. That kind of childhood is laden with stress. That kind of childhood leads to burnout well before adulthood.

According to Dr. Peter Gray,

Rates of depression and anxiety among young people in America have been increasing steadily for the past 50 to 70 years. Today, by at least some estimates, five to eight times as many high school and college students meet the criteria for diagnosis of major depression and/or anxiety disorder as was true half a century or more ago.

He attributes these mental health issues to a decline in free play—which, of course, can only take place when children have downtime.

Further, we have to keep in mind that even if mental health issues don't arise, a lack of downtime means that a child will never learn to entertain herself. Will never be able to live inside her own head. To deal with solitude or quiet time, essential for problem solving and restoration. She may feel she absolutely *has* to be in the company of others, even panicking at the idea of keeping herself amused.

Imagination and creativity—ideas—arise from having time to think, to ponder and reflect, or just let the mind go. A child with downtime will engage in authentic play (self-chosen, self-directed, and without extrinsic goals)—alone and with others. Because play employs divergent thinking (a much-needed 21st century skill), his problem-solving abilities will grow. If he has the time to carry out his plans and bring them to a conclusion, he'll experience the satisfaction that comes from thinking things through and working them out. A child without such time develops only the ability to do what he's told, when he's told to do it. And that child isn't likely to become an adult with initiative.

If we want children to grow up to be resourceful, they will have to start practicing now. On the surface, downtime may look like wasted time. But, below the surface, there's a whole lot going on. And it's below the surface that truly counts!

What's a Teacher to Do?

• You may no longer be allowed to include naptime as part of the day, but it's important to ensure that the children get *some* time to rest. If necessary, use the information in the resources on the next page to advocate for downtime with administrators and parents.

(Continued)

(Continued)

• Also ensure that the children get as much *unstructured* time as possible. Whether that involves free play, recess, or free-choice time, it's important that children learn to do more than follow the directions of adults. A middle school teacher recently told me that her students await instructions for *everything* because they have no idea what to do otherwise.

• If a child is displaying challenging behavior, consider the possibility that she is overtired. If so, allow her some time to do whatever is most restful to her.

• If you find a child daydreaming instead of doing as instructed, resist the urge to scold. You might even ask him to share—privately and in a friendly way—what he was thinking about, thus validating the idea of daydreaming. Remember, too, that we can learn so much from the children when we invite them to share in this way.

Where to Learn More

• You can listen to my conversation about the impact of sleep deprivation on the classroom, with Dr. Mary Sheedy Kurcinka, Dr. James Maas, and two educators, here:

https://www.bamradionetwork.com/track/five-classroom-problems-directly-traceable-to-student-sleep-deprivation/

• I talk with Dr. Mary Helen Immordino-Yang about the value of daydreaming in class in this 12-minute podcast:

https://www.bamradionetwork.com/track/students-daydreaming-in-class-it-s-productive-if/

- Dr. Peter Gray writes about "The Decline of Play and Rise in Children's Mental Disorders" here:

  https://www.psychologytoday.com/us/blog/freedom-learn/201001/the-decline-play-and-rise-in-childrens-mental-disorders

- Read "The Virtues of Daydreaming" here:

  https://www.newyorker.com/tech/frontal-cortex/the-virtues-of-daydreaming

  and "The Upside of Downtime" here:

  https://hbr.org/2012/12/the-upside-of-downtime

- This piece in *Scientific American* explains "Why Your Brain Needs Downtime":

  https://www.scientificamerican.com/article/mental-downtime/

- For an excellent overview on children's need for downtime, read "Is Your Child Getting Enough Real Downtime?":

  https://health.usnews.com/wellness/for-parents/articles/2017-09-28/is-your-child-getting-enough-real-downtime

  It's written by child psychologist Dr. Susan Bartell.

- "Teach Kids to Daydream" is an excellent resource. You'll find it here:

  https://www.theatlantic.com/education/archive/2013/10/teach-kids-to-daydream/280615/

PART II

Teaching With the Body in Mind

CHAPTER 10

Making a Mess of Human Development: The Terrible Impact of Our Choices for Children

I thought I'd heard it all when it came to the lack of movement in children's lives. But when I read a piece about young children falling out of their chairs in classrooms, I literally cried.

My first thought was that this had to be a rare occurrence. But, no; as reported in the article, a first-grade teacher took a tally, and in one week her students fell from their chairs *44 times*. Forty-four times! She said it was like having penguins trying to sit in chairs. A funny image but a not-so-funny situation, especially considering the number of other teachers who have since reported similar incidents to me.

How is this possible? What the heck is going on? Well, it turns out that today's children are getting so little movement that their proprioceptive and vestibular systems are not developing properly.

If you've studied motor or human development, you know that proprioception is awareness of the location of one's body and body parts in relation to the environment. With a properly developed proprioceptive sense, individuals are able to perform such tasks as feeding themselves without having to watch the fork travel to their mouth, or climb a staircase without looking at their feet. The vestibular sense detects gravity and motion, coordinating with the other senses, to create an internal sense of balance. With a properly developed vestibular sense, children will have, in addition to better balance, better visual tracking and self-regulation. When both the proprioceptive and vestibular senses are well developed, children can sit upright and stay that way.

The critical period for development of these senses is before the age of seven. And the best way to promote their development is to allow children to *move*. The wonderful pediatric occupational therapist Angela Hanscom tells us that children are supposed to be moving rapidly in many different directions on a regular basis. That means playing tag, spinning, rolling, hanging upside down, and jumping from high places.

Yesterday's children, who had far more unstructured time and access to such equipment as swings, merry-go-rounds, and monkey bars, had ample opportunity for these experiences. Today's children, many of whom are enrolled in school and centers from infancy, and who are leading highly scheduled, overprotected lives, are being denied these opportunities.

Parents, teachers, and administrators are terrified that children will get hurt, so they discourage, or even forbid, anything that looks like risky play: "Don't run!"—which I once heard a mom exclaim to a child running *uphill on grass*. "Don't spin; you'll get dizzy." "Don't do that; you'll get hurt!" It's no wonder children have trouble sitting still and staying upright!

In fairness, I understand that fear has currently overtaken adults—and it's understandable that they're afraid children will get hurt. Unfortunately, they've been led to believe that nearly everything children do will lead to pain and injury. Because of this, school and city administrators live in another kind of fear—the fear of litigation. As a result, "risky" play rarely takes place on public or school playgrounds these days. Swings, monkey bars, and those wonderful, dizzying merry-go-rounds have been removed. And, as previously mentioned, tag, running, and cartwheels, among other necessary-for-development actions, have been banned at many schools.

As I've repeatedly said in my keynotes, Mother Nature gave us everything we need in order to develop properly. But instead of appreciating and respecting the process of human development, we're thumbing our noses at it! We seem to think we can do better.

But we have to get our priorities straight. We have to stop giving imagined fears more power than the real ones. And the real ones include the impact that all of this nonsense is having on our children. I mean, without spatial awareness and balance, how will children learn to navigate their environment? How will they eventually drive on a busy highway, fit their cars into parking spaces, avoid people on a crowded city sidewalk, or even maneuver shopping carts down narrow grocery store aisles? How will they manage to participate in physical activity in order to keep themselves healthy? They won't have to wait until they're elderly to worry about falls and their resulting injuries. If we're really concerned about children experiencing pain, then we should be really concerned about their lives without well-developed proprioceptive and vestibular senses!

Honestly, who could read about children continually falling out of their chairs and not be shocked and appalled? Who could look at the disturbing changes we've wrought in children and not want to reverse our mistakes? Human development is a miraculous process. Who among us dares to believe that we can improve on it?

What's a Teacher to Do?

• Resist the urge to issue words of caution when a child is spinning or swinging or rolling, that is, being a child. On the contrary, you should encourage it. If a child remains stationary on the playground, urge her to run and jump. Run and jump with her!

(Continued)

(Continued)

• If your school has banned activities such as tag or removed traditional play equipment, use the research to fight back!

• Incorporate brain breaks that involve jumping, turning, and spinning in place. Promote balancing skills by asking children to imagine the lines on the floor are tightropes, and to walk from one end to the other like a high-wire artist.

• If you have a child, or children, falling off chairs, take it seriously. Address the issue with parents. Seek the help of an occupational therapist.

Where to Learn More

• The article to which I refer at the beginning of the chapter can be found here:

https://www.stack.com/a/the-shocking-phenomenon-that-shows-just-how-movement-starved-modern-kids-really-are?fbclid=IwAR2h6ap3etBUhEA-1oKlhrlY318WkCB QBMdJkkubJqn_oogPqEtvfxaKe2A

• There's information about the proprioceptive and vestibular senses, including ways to promote it, in this article called "The Sixth and Seventh Senses":

https://eyaslanding.com/the-vestibular-and-proprioceptive-systems-the-sixth-and-seven-senses/

• Read Angela Hanscom's excellent book, *Balanced and Barefoot: How Unrestricted Outdoor Play Makes for Strong, Confident and Capable Children.*

• Watch Angela's TEDx Talk, only seven and a half minutes long, for better understanding of how the lack of movement in children's lives is impacting the ability to learn:

https://www.ted.com/talks/angela_hanscom_the_real_reason_children_fidget_and_what_we_can_do_about_it

CHAPTER 11

This Just In: Young Children Don't Get Enough Exercise

For as long as I've worked in early childhood education—which is to say, four decades—I've been waiting for the "revolution" in education, as regards an understanding that children need to move. That children do not exist only from the neck up.

When Howard Gardner's Theory of Multiple Intelligences, which included the bodily-kinesthetic intelligence, became well known and popular with educators, I thought the revolution was upon us. Didn't happen.

Then came a whole lot of amazing new brain research with, among other things, significant information about the value of physical activity to learning. Again, I thought the revolution was upon us. Didn't happen.

But once people began hearing about a childhood obesity crisis and all of its horrifying statistics (40 percent of children ages five to eight show at least one heart disease risk factor; one in three American children at risk for type 2 diabetes!), surely the revolution would come. How could it not? Well, as you know…it didn't happen.

In fact, things have only gotten worse. Recess and physical education continue to go the way of the dodo bird, and there's more and more sitting required in classrooms, as our society places greater and greater value on the "head"—and fails to realize how critical exercising the body is to exercising the brain.

As I've beaten my own head against this metaphorical wall for 40 years, I've come to realize that part of the problem, when pleading for kids to have more movement, is the mistaken belief that children, just by virtue of being children, move enough. That hit me again a few years ago when I saw a *USA Today* piece titled "Preschool Kids Starved for Exercise" and its *U.S. News & World Report* counterpart, "Preschoolers Get Too Little Physical Activity in Child Care." Both were citing a study, published in the journal *Pediatrics*, in which the researchers found that children spent only 33 minutes a day playing outside and logged only about 48 minutes per day overall in active play.

But these weren't the first studies determining that pre-schoolers don't get enough exercise. In 2010, the Children's Activity and Movement in Preschools Study (CHAMPS) determined that children enrolled in preschools were engaged in moderate to vigorous physical activity (MVPA) during only 3.4 percent of the day. In 2008, Robert Pate and his colleagues observed 2,000 children and found that those attending preschools were engaged in MVPA during only 2.6 percent of the observation time. During more than 85 percent of that time, the children were engaged in either very light activity or sedentary behaviors.

Since then there have been more and more studies proving the connection between moving and learning. And each of them has been reported as though it was a newsflash!

As we know, once upon a time children ran and skipped, climbed trees, jumped rope, chased bubbles, and rode their bikes for blocks. Before they entered school, it seemed they were never indoors. They and their neighborhood friends ran screaming through each other's yards. They raced each other to the slide and swings, pursued butterflies, and got filthy rolling around on the ground. Then, once they were in school all day (where, by the way, there were two daily recesses), the instant the bell sounded they ran all the way home, shed their good clothes, and were out the door again. They played hopscotch, hide-and-seek, and tag. And they stayed outside until obliged to go in.

Does all of that activity bring to mind what today's children are experiencing? Not even close. Now, according to the National Recreation and Park Association, children devote only *four to seven minutes* a day to unstructured outdoor play, a statistic I find horrifying. Still, most adults imagine that kids are constantly on the move.

Many seem to ignore the reality that children in our current society are often in child care (where, as mentioned, they're not getting enough exercise) from the time they're infants. They start their schooling (where too often adults insist that they sit still) at age three or four. Their days are organized for them practically from dawn to dusk. And they don't walk—let alone run—to and from school. Either they take the bus or their parents drive them. (Kids are not allowed to walk *anywhere* these days.) Once home, even preschool and kindergarten children are expected to do homework now; so, if it's not already dark by the time they get home, they have to use the remaining daylight to get their schoolwork done.

And even if they should find themselves with free time, today's kids are likely spending it with electronics; televisions, computers, and handheld devices are some strong competition for their attention. And, of course, parents often prefer electronics, believing that (1) children are learning more from technology than they can from active play and (2) they need to keep their children inside, safe from the many perceived dangers of the outdoors—despite all statistics to the contrary.

I won't turn this into a lecture on childhood obesity or cite the very long, very frightening list of its health risks. I won't go on and on about the connection between moving and learning, or reiterate the folly of imagining that sitting equals learning. What I will do is emphasize that the human body was made to move— *especially* in the early years—for the sake of both the body *and* the brain.

Guidelines created by the National Association for Sport and Physical Education (NASPE, now part of SHAPE America) recommend that young children get at least 60 minutes of unstructured physical activity each day. Additionally, preschoolers should spend a minimum of 60 minutes a day in structured physical activity. That's not happening for any children I know.

Despite the prevailing belief that this is an issue for families to handle, it's clear to me that it's an area where early childhood professionals can and must make a difference. If today's children are going to spend so much of their time in either child care or school, much of the responsibility *has* to fall to the adults with whom they spend the most time. And, given what's at stake, this is not a responsibility to be taken lightly.

Whether adults live or work with children—or set policies affecting them—my prayer is that they will begin to value the body, even if only for what it can do for the brain. That they will understand the value of movement and realize these are not the "good old days" when, just by virtue of being a child, children were getting all the physical activity they needed.

What's a Teacher to Do?

• The solution is simple: Incorporate more movement into the day, especially of the moderate to vigorous type! If you're concerned about finding the time, or you're under pressure to include more instructional time, Chapter 18 offers "Five Ways to Sneak Movement Into the Curriculum."

• If you want to include more movement in the children's day but don't know where to begin, or don't have the time to create a movement curriculum, use a curriculum that's already available. My *Preschoolers & Kindergartners Moving & Learning* and *Early Elementary Children Moving & Learning* offer lessons plans, with original music.

• You can and should engage with the children outside and encourage more physical activity. You might start a game such as Shadow Tag or Blob Tag and then step out so the game doesn't become adult-directed. You can also circulate among the children, asking questions that prompt them to be more physically active. (For example:

How many steps do you think it is from here to that fence?) You can lead the children in an energetic game of Follow the Leader.

• Share information about the link between physical activity and academic performance, and about physical activity guidelines, with parents and administrators—and, whenever possible, with policymakers!

Where to Learn More

• You can read "Preschool Kids Starved for Exercise" here:

https://www.usatoday.com/story/news/2015/05/18/preschoolers-not-exercising/27396311/

• The *U.S. News & World Report* article can be found here:

https://health.usnews.com/health-news/articles/2015/05/18/preschoolers-arent-getting-enough-physical-activity-in-child-care

• John Ratey's book, *Spark: The Revolutionary New Science of Exercise and the Brain*, although published in 2008, still offers the ultimate explanation of the science behind the mind/body connection.

• Read the research brief, "Active Education: Growing Evidence on Physical Activity and Academic Performance," here:

https://activelivingresearch.org/sites/activelivingresearch.org/files/ALR_Brief_ActiveEducation_Jan2015.pdf

(Continued)

(Continued)

- You can find information regarding SHAPE America's physical activity guidelines here: https://www.shapeamerica.org/standards/guidelines/. Included on the site is information about *Active Start: A Statement of Physical Activity Guidelines for Children From Birth to Age 5* (https://www.shapeamerica.org/standards/guidelines/activestart.aspx) and a statement of guidelines for children 5–12 (https://www.shapeamerica.org/standards/guidelines/pa-children-5-12.aspx).

- My book, *Great Games for Young Children*, offers more than 100 games that can be played both inside and outside.

CHAPTER 12

The Link Between Movement and Challenging Behavior

When you think of children in motion, do you imagine them bouncing off the walls? Fear of losing control of the children is a primary reason teachers are disinclined to encourage movement in their settings.

It's true that movement can generate a lot of energy. But you might be surprised to learn that *lack* of movement is far more likely to create challenging behavior in your setting! It's when children are forced to sit still—an undertaking that certainly doesn't come naturally to them—that problems arise.

As I've mentioned, just like any other young animal, young children were born to move. When we remove that option, they become restless and frustrated. And no good can come from restless, frustrated children. They fidget. They act out. When they're told over and over again to sit still, they begin to feel like failures—as early as three and four years old—because they can't do what this important adult is asking them to do. When a three-year-old child repeatedly has notes sent home because he's not able to sit still (true story), what happens to his natural joy? How can he comply, when he's not developmentally equipped to do so? How can he see school as a place he wants to be? As a place that's safe? And, because he has no choice but to be there, how can he *not* act out?

Too often we see fidgeting and the need to move as misbehavior (more about this in Chapter 16). But the late Fritz Bell, founder of Creative Classrooms in New Hampshire, once said, "We can keep telling the children, 'Sit still!' Or we can accept that they're children and acknowledge what comes naturally to them."

If we want *engaged*, as opposed to submissive, children we have to understand and embrace the *nature* of children.

Sure, we've all seen those old black-and-white photos of classrooms from years gone by—the ones with children seated primly in neat rows. Having "control" of the kids and requiring them to learn via their eyes, their ears, and the seat of their pants was perceived as the best way to provide an education. And the theory may have been logical back then; they didn't have any research to prove otherwise. But today we do.

Today we have research demonstrating that sitting in a chair *increases fatigue*. Educator Eric Jensen has written extensively about this issue. He confirms that sitting for more than 10 minutes at a time reduces our awareness of physical and emotional sensations. Also, the pressure on spinal discs is 30 percent greater while sitting than while standing. None of this contributes to optimal health or learning. Nor does it contribute to optimal behavior. In *Learning With the Body in Mind*, Jensen writes, "These problems reduce concentration and attention, and ultimately result in discipline problems." So, why would we want children to sit more often?

Jensen is just one of many educators and researchers to ring the warning bell about the folly of sitting to learn. As far back as 1929, Alfred North Whitehead wrote, "I lay it down as an educational axiom that in teaching you will come to grief as soon as you forget that your pupils have bodies."

More recently, an educator told me the same thing in the simplest of terms. He said, "If you don't let them move, you've already lost them."

I would add that if you don't let them move, you're going to see more challenging behavior.

**What's a
Teacher to Do?**

- I do know that the idea of moving children can be scary. That's why it's important to have a plan. The first step in that plan is to implement rules specifically for movement. The two most important rules are: *We will respect one another's personal space* and *We will move with as little noise as possible.* These should not just be decreed but practiced—in as playful a way as possible. For example, help children understand the concept of personal space by inviting them to move around the room as though in bubbles, challenging them not to get close enough to burst anyone else's bubble.

- Use circle games to foster a feeling of community. This is especially important for marginalized students. Zaretta Hammond, in *Culturally Responsive Teaching and the Brain*, tells us that they "need to feel affirmed and included as valued members of a learning community." In a circle, each individual is significant. When everyone in the circle has a role and responsibility, a feeling of community grows. This won't necessarily happen in circle times that require the children to sit in a certain position and simply listen. Rather, it is active participation by all that creates community. And when the children have a sense of community, they have less reason to act out.

- Similarly, cooperative games promote prosocial skills, while competition fosters antisocial skills. When you have friendlier feelings in your setting, again, the children have less reason to act out. Cooperative activities also develop trust among partners and groups, and trust increases feelings of connection in the brain.

- Monitor energy levels. Too much energy can result in frustrating, unproductive, unmanageable experiences. Too little energy, however, can have comparable results. Tired children tend to display irritability and off-task behavior. If you plan movement activities when the children are well

(Continued)

(Continued)

rested and not overstimulated from another activity and alternate livelier and quieter activities, you should be able to prevent frenzy and fatigue.

Where to Learn More

- My book, *Acting Out!: Avoid Behavior Challenges With Active Learning Games & Activities*, offers additional tips, along with circle games, cooperative activities, brain breaks, and more.

- As an alternative, you could enroll in my online course called "Avoid Challenging Behavior in Your Early Childhood Setting," found here:

  https://raepica.teachable.com/p/avoid-challenging-behavior-in-early-childhood-settings

- *Think of Something Quiet*, written by the late Clare Cherry, has been around since 1981 but perhaps now is more relevant and needed than ever. It offers early childhood educators strategies for achieving a low-stress classroom environment.

- You can't go wrong with Eric Jensen's *Learning With the Body in Mind: The Scientific Basis for Energizers, Movement, Play, and Physical Education*.

- Listen to this conversation on the Not Just Cute podcast about how movement helps us avoid behavior challenges:

  https://notjustcute.com/podcast/episode29/

CHAPTER 13

Teaching the Whole Child Means Addressing Physical Development, Too

I may not *accept* the fact that motor skills don't receive as much attention and respect as literacy and numeracy skills. But given the prevailing belief that the mind and body are separate entities—and that the functions of the mind are superior to the functions of the body—I do understand that attitude isn't likely to change anytime soon. Still, I keep plugging away in hopes that early childhood professionals and parents will actually take this message to heart: Motor skills matter to the "whole child," too!

What's fascinating is that a study involving parents and teachers in 15 countries found that the majority believe the development of motor skills is important for their children. However, they evidently also assume motor skill development happens without adult intervention—because neither the parents nor the teachers felt it was their responsibility to promote it. Nor did they feel it was the responsibility of the other group!

Most people, it seems, imagine that children acquire motor skills automatically as their bodies develop—that it's a natural, "magical" process that occurs along with maturation. Unfortunately, this is an easy assumption to make. After all, one day the infant rolls over by herself, eventually starts to crawl, and then suddenly rises up onto hands and knees and begins creeping.

Somewhere around her first birthday or so, with only a little assistance and a lot of enthusiastic encouragement from adults, she takes her first steps. And then, almost before you know it, she's off and running.

So, it certainly *appears* that motor skills miraculously occur and then take care of themselves. And, to a certain extent, it's true. However, maturation takes care of only part of the process— the part that allows a child to execute most movement skills at an immature level.

What does an *immature level* mean? Consider the phrase "She throws like a girl" and the even more insulting phrase "*He* throws like a girl." Regardless of which gender the words are directed at, they refer to a child who hasn't achieved a mature performance level for the skill of throwing. Something about the child's form isn't quite right. And, believe it or not, it can happen with such basic motor skills as walking and running. Perhaps you've even observed a child who hasn't quite mastered the ability to move limbs in perfect opposition, or whose feet roll in, baby toes lifting off the ground.

The truth is, thanks to the mistaken notion that children don't need help in this area—along with today's sedentary life-styles—a *lot* of children never achieve mature patterns for many motor skills. As evidence of this, as reported in 2012, a British study found that almost a third of four- and five-year-olds struggle with such basic movements as crawling and balancing on one leg. An earlier study, in Australia, reported that fewer than 10 percent of the 1,200 children observed were able to run correctly.

Whether or not you think highly of motor skills, this is truly upsetting. And we can't kid ourselves that this is happening only in other countries.

Never mind the fact that movement contributes to improved academic performance. (I can get pretty tired of justifying the actions of the body in terms of what they have to offer the brain.)

The ability to perform motor skills is related directly to physical fitness. And, considering the health hazards for the unfit, this is one area that matters more than literacy or numeracy.

A *competent* mover will gladly keep moving. A child or an adult (poor movement habits track from childhood) who feels physically awkward and uncoordinated is simply going to avoid movement at all costs. There's no mystery as to why research shows that children lacking in movement fundamentals are more sedentary than peers of the same age who are skilled movers.

Additionally, children (even preschoolers) tend to be movement "snobs"—a fact that impacts both their social and emotional development. Physical skill has been positively associated with peer acceptance and leadership among adolescents and elementary-school students. Even five- and six-year-olds with high levels of motor skills tend to be more popular than those with the lowest levels, especially among boys.

It makes sense, really: the more skilled children are, the more they engage in physical play, which grants them greater opportunities for social interaction. And along with it all come confidence and higher levels of self-esteem.

You likely sense that I worry quite a bit about our children and their future. Often, that worry involves their social/emotional development. But, even if we did everything right concerning other domains of development, if we neglect children's physical development, they're in for a world of hurt. Because not being able to crawl or balance or run properly affects the *whole child*—which means it will affect the whole *adult*, too.

What's a Teacher to Do?

• I realize that when I talk about this kind of thing, early childhood professionals get nervous. I can *feel* the tension as they fear that I'm asking them, on top of *everything else they do*, to be motor development experts, too. But not to worry. All I'm asking is that you apply the same level of observation to the children's physical abilities as you do to other areas of your program.

(Continued)

(Continued)

- If you see a child who appears to have motor delays, or who makes no improvement in motor skill development over time, take action—whether that's working with the child yourself or bringing in the expert help of a physical education teacher or occupational therapist.

- Help parents see the importance of the physical realm and its relationship to the social/emotional and cognitive domains.

- Implement the suggestions in Chapter 18, "Five Ways to Sneak Movement Into the Curriculum."

Where to Learn More

- Here's the link to the British study to which I referred:

  https://www.dailymail.co.uk/health/article-2229567/The-children-held-school-lazy-lifestyles-mean-t-stand-leg.html

- "Make Active Play Part of Your Day" outlines some of the health hazards of sedentary behaviors:

  https://www.raepica.com/2017/08/make-active-play-part-day/

- Learn about a study titled "Associations Between Sedentary Behavior and Motor Coordination in Children" here:

  https://onlinelibrary.wiley.com/doi/abs/10.1002/ajhb.22310

- Listen to an 11-minute podcast called "Solving the Growing Physical Activity Crisis":

  https://www.bamradionetwork.com/track/solving-the-growing-physical-activity-crisis/

- Another relevant podcast is "Fitting Fitness Into the Curriculum":

  https://www.bamradionetwork.com/track/fitting-fitness-into-the-curriculum/

CHAPTER 14

The Magic of Cross-Lateral Movement

Cross-lateral movements, like a baby's crawling, activate both hemispheres [of the brain] in a balanced way. These activities work both sides of the body evenly and involve coordinated movements of both eyes, both ears, both hands and both feet as well as balanced core muscles. When both eyes, both ears, both hands and feet are being used equally, the corpus callosum orchestrating these processes between the two hemispheres becomes more highly developed. Because both hemispheres and all four lobes are activated, cognitive functioning is heightened and ease of learning increases.

Those are the words of neurophysiologist Carla Hannaford, writing in *Smart Moves: Why Learning Is Not All in Your Head*.

And here are the words of a reading specialist who once, very publicly, as we were consulting for the *Sesame Street* Research Department, objected to a story I told about the role of movement in learning to read: *The only way to learn to read is by reading*.

Regardless of that contention, I frequently tell the story that Dr. Hannaford relates in *Smart Moves*: that of Todd, who at

16 years old was still unable to read, despite the time, effort, and money his parents had invested in helping him learn. All that changed when his mother discovered Brain Gym and learned about the Cross Crawl, an activity in which an individual alternately touches right elbow to left knee and left elbow to right knee.

To make sure Todd performed this exercise, the whole family cross-crawled every morning before he went to school and every evening before he went to bed. *Six weeks later,* Todd was reading—at grade level. He even went on to join the basketball team, which previously wasn't possible for him because, even though he was tall, he hadn't been able to dribble a ball! And following high school, Todd went to college, where he received a degree in biology.

Now, it may seem like a coincidence that after six weeks of cross-crawling, Todd was suddenly able to read. This is what the reading specialist contended. But if we review the words that open this piece, we see that cross-lateral movements activate both sides of the brain and stimulate the corpus callosum, which is the matter between the two hemispheres. Dr. Hannaford tells us that Todd had all of the information he needed in the hemispheres of his brain; the two hemispheres simply weren't communicating across the corpus callosum. Doing the Cross Crawl, an activity that requires crossing the body's midline (the invisible line running from the head to the toes and dividing the body into right and left sides), opened up the pathways of communication. And, presto; Todd could read!

Of course, it's not surprising that the reading specialist was so adamant. In the first place, she was defending her job. In the second place—and this is the big issue—she couldn't see the link between mind and body. How could reading, an activity of the mind, possibly be impacted by the actions of the body? But the actions of the body are continually impacting the activities of the mind.

Evidence for this can be found in the discoveries of friend and colleague Dr. Marjorie Corso, a now-retired physical education specialist, who conducted research on how body-space awareness transfers to paper-space awareness. One of her surprising findings was that children who can't cross the body's vertical midline tend to focus on the vertical of the paper, sometimes writing or drawing down the vertical center of the page and sometimes changing the pencil to the other hand at the midpoint of the paper. A teacher told me recently that she's also seen children switch from one side of the desk to the other in order to keep writing across the paper. All are clear signs of the connection between mind and body.

Unfortunately, I'm not one of those quick thinkers—you know, like Robin Williams was, with his lightning-fast wit. I tend to replay conversations in my head over and over again and finally formulate what I should have said somewhere between three hours and three days later. And what I realized I should have asked that reading specialist was, "How is it possible to learn to do something you can't do by doing it?" I would really love the answer to that.

I realize we have a longstanding history of believing the body has absolutely nothing to do with how the mind works. But why should that be more difficult to believe than the possibility that somebody can learn to do something they can't do by doing it?

What's a Teacher to Do?

• Watch for children who have difficulty crossing the midline. Signs of this include using the left hand for activities on the left side of the body, and vice versa; switching hands halfway through a task; and rotating the trunk to avoid reaching across the body.

• Todd's story shows that it's not too late for cross-lateral movement to work its magic. Get young children on the floor, pretending to be kitties, puppies, snakes, and spiders! Chances are good that, among other benefits, reading and writing will come more easily.

• If you happen to work with infants, make sure they get plenty of tummy time.

(Continued)

(Continued)

• Encourage children to cross the midline. You might hand them objects that they must reach across the body to retrieve. Invite the children to show you with their arms how windshield wipers work. Play a game in which the children, standing or sitting in line, each must pass a ball to the child behind by turning her or his body. Hand out scarves or ribbon sticks and encourage the children to create circles or sideways figure-eights (the infinity sign) in the air in front of them. Use cross-lateral activities such as the Cross Crawl for brain breaks, or while the children have to be waiting in line.

• If your efforts to help a child cross the midline don't improve the situation, advise the child's parents and refer the parents to an occupational therapist.

Where to Learn More

• Carla Hannaford's *Smart Moves: Why Learning Is Not All in Your Head* is my favorite professional book. I wish every educator and parent could read it.

• For activity ideas involving crossing the midline, check out my YouTube video, "Emergent Literacy: Why Cross-Lateral Movement Matters!":

https://www.youtube.com/watch?v=yrYMIcXC9Yw&t=11s

• To learn about Brain Gym:

www.braingym.org

• For more on the mind–body connection, read "Do the Children in Your Classrooms Have Bodies?":

https://www.raepica.com/2017/12/mind-body-connection/

- This Pinterest page offers ideas and resources:

  https://www.pinterest.com/growhandsonkids/crossing-midline-activities/

- "Effect of Ability to Cross Midline on Performance of Handwriting" can be downloaded here:

  https://scholarworks.wmich.edu/ot_posters/39/

CHAPTER 15

No Fine Motor Skills? What's the Big Deal?

Everywhere I go, whether in person or virtually, early childhood teachers tell me that young children are seriously lacking in fine motor control these days.

The children can't grip a crayon or paintbrush. The children can't use scissors. The children don't know how to hold a pencil.

On and on it goes, much of it coming from kindergarten and first-grade teachers. They report that their young charges don't even have the strength to tear a piece of paper or take the paper off a straw! Although it shocks me, it doesn't actually surprise me.

There are two major reasons why. The first is that the little ones are far more likely to be holding a digital device these days than a crayon or pair of scissors. Go to any restaurant where families dine—or to a doctor's office, or anywhere else parents and kids gather—and you won't see a child coloring while the family waits. They're not even talking to each other because they're all too engaged with their own cell phones or tablets. If they're using any muscles at all—besides their poor, tired eyes—it's simply to swipe a screen.

Children who grow up swiping instead of coloring, cutting, and painting do not develop the fine motor skills they need to hold a pencil and write. To button and unbutton their clothes. To properly hold a utensil for eating. To grasp, squeeze, and release a stapler or bottle of glue. To pull up a zipper!

The second reason this trend doesn't surprise me is that children are spending so little time crawling, running, jumping, or climbing these days. To those unfamiliar with motor skill development, that might seem like a strange connection. But, here's the thing: Control over the body develops from the top to the bottom of the body, from the inside of the body (trunk) to the outside (extremities), and from the large muscles to the small muscles. That means that until the trunk and large muscles are matured, the small ones in the hands won't fully develop. This is nature's plan. This is immutable. And this is why I've heard it said that the best way to help children learn to write is by letting them climb trees or swing on the monkey bars.

Lack of fine motor skills may not seem like a big deal to those parents and teachers who see children's future success in terms of what they will be able to do digitally. But we only have to stop for a moment and ponder the frustration of being unable to unbutton a shirt with ease. To fill out a form with a pen. Or to manipulate a knife and fork—particularly in public.

A stronger argument, especially when addressing the issue with parents, is that children without fine motor skills have very little chance to become successful chefs, fashion designers, or house flippers. With the popularity of such television shows as *Top Chef* and *Chopped*, we've witnessed the need for expert knife work. *Project Runway* has brought to light the fine motor control required of sketching, cutting, and sewing. And anyone who's watched Chip Gaines on *Fixer Upper* has observed the success that can result from swinging a hammer and driving a nail.

Becoming athletic may also be problematic. It's difficult to manipulate a baseball, golf club, or tennis racket when you don't have enough strength in your hands and fingers even to tear a piece of paper.

And then there are the surgeons, whose work absolutely requires them to have well-developed fine motor skills. There are few professions, in truth, that require as much precise handiwork as that of a surgeon.

Of course, I had no proof that such professions would in reality pose a problem for children lacking in fine motor development. It was merely theory on my part—until a colleague sent me an article quoting Roger Kneebone, a professor of surgical education in London. In it he contends, "New medical students have spent so much time on screens that they lack vital practical skills necessary to conduct life-saving operations."

Dr. Kneebone is part of a campaign working to return more hands-on creative subjects to the curriculum, which he states have a positive effect on the tactile skills necessary for a career in medicine or science. And, I might add, in cooking, fashion, carpentry, or sports.

I don't know what it will take before adults realize that the "old stuff" (crayons, play dough, blocks) holds more value than the shiny new digital stuff—with fewer inherent dangers. Sadly, for now it appears that things are heading in the wrong direction. A 2019 study reported that screen time for the under-two set more than doubled from 1997 to 2014, with the little ones spending 3.05 hours a day in front of screens. I can barely stand to imagine what all that screen time replaced in their lives, or the host of health-related issues that will result from it.

Unfortunately, it may take a good long while before health and career-related issues become severe enough that an "aha" moment occurs. My fear is that it will be too late by then for an entire generation of children.

In the meantime, perhaps we can hasten that aha moment by pointing out to parents and policymakers that hours spent glued to the screen will do nothing to help develop and refine those tactile skills to which Dr. Kneebone referred. Those fine motor skills that will enable children to become capable of handling the life and professional skills requiring them.

What's a Teacher to Do?

• Pediatric occupational therapist Christy Isbell recommends that young children have plenty of appropriate materials and objects with which to practice their fine motor skills. These include "a wide variety of open-ended materials such as paper, drawing utensils, glue, clay, and small blocks." Of course, you must also give children the time to draw, mold, cut, and build!

(Continued)

(Continued)

• Dr. Isbell additionally counsels that children "spend more time playing with manipulatives than practicing writing skills"—because if young children are pushed to write before their hands are physically ready, it may have a negative impact.

• When the children are working with blocks (and please make sure they do), if necessary, begin with larger, wooden blocks. You can then gradually downsize them.

• Despite the dearth of such play equipment as monkey bars and jungle gyms, you can ensure that children get as much opportunity as possible to run and jump and build their large muscles.

• Do your best to educate parents about the need for their children to continue to climb trees and swing from their limbs. Parents need to understand that the risk of *not* performing such activities is much greater than engaging in them.

Where to Learn More

• Christy Isbell's book *Mighty Fine Motor Fun: Fine Motor Activities for Young Children* offers the support and tools teachers need to teach fine motor skills.

• A second resource is *Basics of Fine Motor Skills: Developmental Activities for Kids*, written by Heather Greutman and intended for parents, educators, and therapists.

- Listen to "Fine Motor Skills: What Are They? Why Are They Too Important to Overlook?," a 10-minute podcast featuring Christy Isbell, kindergarten teacher Allison Sampish, and early childhood expert Deborah Stewart:

  http://www.bamradionetwork.com/educators-channel/ 774-fine-motor-skills-what-are-they-why-are-they-too- important-to-overlook

- A second relevant podcast is "Introducing Writing Skills to Young Children," with pediatric occupational therapist Angela Hanscom and early childhood expert Amanda Morgan:

  http://www.bamradionetwork.com/student-centric- strategies/4287-introducing-writing-skills-to-very-young- children

- For information on the screen-time study, read "Screen Time for Kids Under 2 More Than Doubles, Study Finds":

  https://www.cnn.com/2019/02/18/health/kids-screen-time- tv-study/index.html

CHAPTER 16

Fidgety, Wiggly Kids? Here's What You Need to Know

Do you find yourself asking certain children to *please sit still* over and over again? Or, at the very least, are you internally begging them to *stop fidgeting*?

There's no doubt that fidgeting can be distracting. But too often it's seen as *misbehaving*. Many a child has been moved up or down on those abominable behavior charts and, unable to comply with the teacher's wishes, made to feel like a failure at the ripe old age of four or five. And that should never be the case.

Nor should it be the case that a child gets coded as having attention issues, or labeled as having attention deficit hyperactivity disorder (ADHD), simply because he or she can't sit still in school.

As I've said, children in general are not meant to sit still. But for some children, sitting still is simply unachievable. I know—because I'm a world-class fidgeter. And although my concentration isn't as strong as I'd like it to be, I don't have ADHD or other attention issues. Nor am I "misbehaving." I just can't be still.

At the movies, I'm the one crossing and uncrossing my legs. At home in the evenings, staying in one position on the couch is impossible. And the more tired I am, the more impossible staying still becomes. In the office, during an important phone conversation during which I need to think more clearly, I typically pace the room. At airports waiting to board a plane, I'm the one swaying side to side. I can't say exactly why I feel the need to sway, but I do know it's self-soothing—and nobody had better ask me to stop doing it!

Pediatric occupational therapist Angela Hanscom contends—rightly so—that children simply don't move enough and that's why they're fidgeting more than ever. That lack of movement, she says, has resulted in children having underdeveloped balance systems and strength. She writes:

> *Children are going to class with bodies that are less prepared to learn than ever before. With sensory systems not quite working right, they are asked to sit and pay attention. Children naturally start fidgeting, in order to get the movement their body so desperately needs and is not getting enough of to "turn their brain on." What happens when the children start fidgeting? We ask them to sit still and pay attention; therefore, their brain goes back to "sleep."*

In a study from 2008, researchers found that children in general need to move in order to focus during a complicated mental task. Dr. Mark Rapport, the study supervisor, explained that this is why children must move while reading or doing math but are able to sit still while watching a movie.

Of course, there will be some fidgeters in your class for whom attention disorders *are* an issue. A 2015 study reported that for these children, hyperactive movements—like moving and spinning in the chair—also meant better performance on tasks requiring concentration. Dr. Dustin Sarver, the ADHD researcher who led the study, said that when the kids were moving, they were increasing their alertness, and that slight physical movements "wake up" the nervous system in much the same way that Ritalin does.

According to Dr. Sarver, when we tell a kid, "Sit down, don't move, stop tapping, stop bouncing," the child is spending all his mental energy concentrating on that rule. And that doesn't allow him to concentrate on whatever task we're asking him to do.

Yes, fidgeting can be distracting. But isn't it better to let children squirm if it means they can think more clearly? To have them wiggling as opposed to medicated?

What's a Teacher to Do?

• The solution, for *all* children, is to ensure that they have more opportunities to move and play in the classroom. For example, use learning centers through which the children must rotate. Refer to Chapter 18 for more ideas.

• Never withhold recess as punishment, *especially* if the "infraction" is fidgeting! Recess should be held at least once a day for all children.

• If you can get standing desks for your classroom, do it! In one study, researchers equipped four first-grade classrooms in Texas with standing desks. Although the desks came equipped with stools, 70 percent of the children never sat; and the remaining 30 percent stood most of the time. The result was that standing increased attention, alertness, engagement, and on-task behavior. That's a teacher's dream!

• In lieu of standing desks, replace traditional chairs with balance balls.

• If you don't have standing desks or balance balls, simply allow children to stand as needed. There's just no reason to force children to stay seated, especially when they're more likely to be attentive while standing.

• Wrap bike inner tubes around the legs of chairs, allowing children to bounce their legs as needed.

• Put children who frequently need to move on the outside of desk clusters so they can move without distracting others. Or simply instruct children who need to stand (or sway) always to do so on the perimeters of the classroom.

(Continued)

(Continued)

• Make stress balls or coloring books available to children. Just because they're using them doesn't mean they're not paying attention to you. A participant at one of my keynotes approached me afterwards to show me what she'd drawn while listening to me speak. Despite having created a lovely drawing, it was evident she had indeed been listening.

• Stay open to unusual solutions. One teacher told me absolutely nothing had worked until she received permission from a child's parents to let him chew gum in class.

Where to Learn More

• You can read Angela Hansom's piece, "The Real Reason Why Kids Fidget," here:

https://www.huffpost.com/entry/the-real-reason-why-kids-fidget_b_5586265

• Read "Kids Who Can't Sit Still," which references the 2008 study, here:

http://www.nea.org/tools/47003.htm

• The 2015 study headed by Dr. Dustin Sarver is explained here:

https://www.umc.edu/news/News_Articles/2015/April/Researcher–Hyperactive-movements-help-ADHD-children-learn.html

• Dr. Dustin Sarver and Angela Hanscom are guests on this podcast episode titled "Why Students Fidget in Class: Abnormal and Distracting or Normal and Desirable?":

https://www.bamradionetwork.com/track/why-students-fidget-in-class-abnormal-and-distracting-or-normal-and-desirable-2/

CHAPTER 17

Let's Do Away With Crisscross-Applesauce

How long can you sit in the same position before you need to move? For me, the answer is: about 20 seconds! As I suggested in the last chapter, unless I'm deeply, deeply engaged in something, I will change positions multiple times or start to fidget. Even while watching something absolutely fascinating on TV, I'm going to go from sitting with my legs folded underneath me to sitting with my legs stretched onto the coffee table to lying on my right side to lying on my left side. And that's all during an hour-long program.

In other words, staying completely still is not my best event. And I'm a long way from being a toddler or a preschooler and among the most active segment of our population.

I've written many times, including in the previous chapter, about the folly of requiring children to sit still in order to learn. But requiring them to sit crisscross-applesauce—cross-legged, with the back straight and hands in the lap—as is so often done during circle or story time, brings the issue to a whole new level.

I have no inkling when sitting like this became a "thing." The idea, of course, is that the children will pay greater attention to the task at hand. That they'll be more capable of listening. But wiggling and moving don't necessarily mean that they're not. In fact, being required to sit like this may mean they pay even *less* attention, because crisscross-applesauce is a particularly challenging position. And that means it can require the majority of a child's concentration.

When sitting crisscross-applesauce became one of the major dictates of the early childhood setting, it gave the child who's incapable of complying one more chance to be seen as misbehaving. To break the rules. But I propose that we examine why such rules exist in the first place—rules that run contrary to what we know about children and, now, about fidgeting. If we understand that children are much more likely to be engaged when they're comfortable, why insist that they assume a position that perhaps isn't comfortable at all, often for many long minutes at a time?

So, what are the alternatives? Well, as pediatric occupational therapist Christy Isbell once said, in a podcast for BAM!radio Network:

> *Who's to say we have to sit down to learn? Why can't we stand to learn? Why can't we lay on the floor on our tummies to learn? Why can't we sit in the rocking chair to learn? There are lots of other simple movement strategies. Just changing the position can make a big difference.*

One major benefit to offering the children options is that they can choose the one that best meets their needs. Because they're given that responsibility and choice, they will take the decision seriously, and there will be fewer actual behavioral issues. This is how self-regulation is acquired—not by being ordered to sit still.

Often, as I've previously mentioned, early childhood teachers argue that they must get children used to sitting because the children are going to have to sit in their later school years.

Unfortunately, it's true that until policymakers begin paying attention to the research and opt for an education system that aligns with how kids learn, children will have to become accustomed to sitting in school. But requiring them to sit still in an uncomfortable position in early childhood is similar to the expectation that, ready or not, they will read by the end of kindergarten.

Learning to sit is a *process* put in place by nature. And that process involves *movement*, which allows children to develop their proprioceptive and vestibular systems. Only when these senses have been developed will children be able to sit still.

Surely, maintaining the tradition of crisscross-applesauce is less important than providing children with the best possible opportunities to learn. Let's do away with it! After all, whacking kids with rulers also was once a painful tradition. Let's make crisscross-applesauce just as outdated as that one.

What's a Teacher to Do?

• It's so important not to jump to the conclusion that a child has attention issues simply because she can't sit still. Not long ago I came across an illustration of five kittens, four of which were sitting perfectly still and looking at the camera. The fifth was behind the others and playing with something that had caught his attention. The label on the photo said something to the effect of, "Guess which kitten has ADD." It's funny, yes. But we have to ask ourselves why the one kitten who's doing what comes *naturally* to kittens is labeled as having ADD. It's the *other* kittens—the ones lined up like soldiers—who aren't behaving naturally!

• As indicated in the previous chapter, you might simply allow children to stand or walk as needed, or to engage in a quiet activity, like coloring, as you read a story. You can and should designate a specified area within which the children are allowed to stand or color, and that area should be within the circle. If you're going to allow children to walk, designate a larger, outside circle that will help prevent the other children from being distracted.

• If a child is unable to sit still while you're reading a story or otherwise attempting to engage him, remember not to take it personally. Once you get to know each child as an individual, you'll be able to determine who might need a stress ball, for example, or to sit on a balance ball.

(Continued)

(Continued)

- If you find yourself distracted by the children's movement, it's important to remember that, as adults, we should be better able to make adjustments to our thinking than young children are to behaviors that are beyond their control.

Where to Learn More

- Listen to the above-mentioned podcast, "Teaching Strategies: Handling Young Students Who Just Won't Sit Still":

  https://www.bamradionetwork.com/track/teaching-strategieshandling-young-students-who-just-wont-sit-still-2/

- More thoughts and recommendations are available on this blog post written by an educator:

  https://applesandbananaseducation.com/criss-cross-applesauce-obsolete/

- Here are even more thoughts on the topic from early childhood educator Deborah Stewart:

  https://teachpreschool.org/2019/07/02/i-cannot-sit-crisscross-applesauce-with-my-hands-in-my-lap/

CHAPTER 18

Five Ways to Sneak Movement Into the Curriculum

I t's really sad to have to talk about "sneaking" movement into the children's day. Once upon a time, young children in an early childhood setting spent *most* of their days moving. Unless they were listening to a story or creating a work of art, they rarely sat.

Unfortunately, that's not the case today. I hate to tell you how many times teachers in my presentations have said that administrators have reprimanded them for doing an activity with the children that everyone in the early childhood profession should know is developmentally appropriate—and important!

I know it's hard to rebel—especially when your livelihood relies on your being compliant with the rules—no matter how ludicrous those rules might be. But we have to do whatever we can for the children. If that means closing your classroom door, or sneaking movement in wherever you can, then that's what has to be done.

So, here are my suggestions for how you can manage that.

First, group or circle time provides the perfect opportunity for movement. As hinted at in the last chapter, there is no law that says everything you do during group time must involve seated, stationary children. Even if you're reading them a story, allowing them to move freely while listening will ensure they don't get restless. They'll also have the opportunity to feel the rhythm of the words you're reading. And if they're allowed to act out the story, they'll better remember its characters, plot, and sequence.

Group time is also the perfect opportunity for you to facilitate an actual movement activity or two. An example would be something like Simon Says, which is an excellent listening and body-parts activity. If you play it without the elimination process, the children will get much more practice. To make this happen, divide the group into two circles. When a child moves without Simon's permission, she or he simply leaves her or his original circle and goes to the other one. Then, "Simon" can make requests such as the following:

- Raise your arms.
- Touch your head.
- Stand up tall.
- Touch your toes.
- Touch your shoulders.
- Pucker up your lips.
- Stand on one foot.
- Place your hands on your hips.
- Bend and touch your knees.
- Close (open) your eyes.
- Reach for the sky.
- Give yourself a hug!

Eventually, you can make the game more challenging by incorporating such "difficult" body parts as elbows, wrists, ankles, temples, and shins.

This may seem like just fun and games, but body-part identification falls under the content area of science for young children, and listening skills are components of both music and emergent literacy.

Brain breaks are a must if you want to avoid restlessness and off-task behavior. And as we know by now, they're also necessary for learning, as sitting increases fatigue and reduces concentration. Knowing that the learning brain can only absorb information for a handful of minutes at a time, why would we want the children to sit for more than a handful of minutes at a time?

For a brain break, you can invite the children to do something as simple as bending and stretching. For instance, have them show you the following:

- Stretch as though you're picking fruit from a tall tree.
- Flop like a rag doll.
- Stretch as though you're waking up and yawning first thing in the morning.
- Bend over as though to tie shoes.
- Stretch to put something on a high shelf.
- Bend to pat a dog; an even smaller dog, or a cat.
- Stretch to shoot a basketball through a hoop.
- Bend to pick up a coin from the floor.
- Stretch as though you're climbing a ladder.
- Bend to pick vegetables or flowers from a garden.

The concepts of up, down, high, and low fall under the headings of both mathematics and art.

Outdoor time, of course, is an obvious time for movement. Outside, children will:

- burn the most calories;
- have the chance to practice and refine emerging physical skills;
- invent games and rules;
- develop their social skills; and
- engage in loud, boisterous behaviors that aren't possible or welcome indoors.

All of this doesn't even take into account the fact that the outside light contributes to our happiness factor, to improved vision, and to productivity. So, the children should get *at least* one outdoor recess per day—rain or shine or temps below freezing!

Using movement across the curriculum is suggestion number four. As we know, young children are experiential learners—and the more senses they use in the learning process, the more information they retain. For these two reasons alone, worksheets are not the way to help children learn.

Finally, there is no better way to sneak in active learning than through transitions. The children are going to be moving anyway, and they'll learn a heck of a lot more by pretending to be astronauts floating in outer space than by walking in a line "holding bubbles" in their mouths.

Here are a couple of transition activities and the content areas they connect to:

- Floating weightlessly like astronauts = social studies (occupations), math (the quantitative concept of *lightly*), and emergent literacy (word comprehension)
- Follow the Leader = emergent literacy and art (physically replicating what the eyes see)
- Moving in different shapes and at different levels = math and art
- Moving like stalking cats = science (animals), math (the concept of *lightly*), and emergent literacy (word comprehension, specifically adjectives)

It is truly sad that we have to justify developmentally appropriate practice. It's also absurd, considering that the research is on our side. But until the policymakers see the light, we can practice "civil disobedience" and sneak movement into the curriculum so the young children in our care can get a *real* education.

What's a Teacher to Do?

• To add extra "credibility" to your movement activities, you can accompany them with children's books. For example, to accompany a body-parts activity like Simon Says, you might choose *Bend and Stretch: Learning About Your Bones and Muscles*, by Pamela Hill Nettleton. Another possibility is *Eyes, Nose, Fingers, and Toes* by Judy Hindley. To help create additional appreciation for the outdoors, you might read *Our Great Big Backyard* by Laura Bush and Jenna Bush Hager.

- Managing behavior challenges is of great importance to educators and can be used to make a case in favor of movement activities. One of the many benefits of movement experiences is that children become acquainted with the concept of personal space. Once familiar and respectful of it, such incidents as sitting too close and kicking one another will be minimized.

- Also as it relates to behavior challenges, you can use the information in Chapter 12 to advocate for movement in the classroom.

- If, heaven forbid, recess has been eliminated in your setting, take some of your learning outside and make sure as much of it as possible is active! For example, if you're studying transportation, the children would have more space outside to demonstrate various modes.

- If an administrator should pop into your room while the children are creating letter shapes with their bodies or measuring things with their hands, you may have some explaining to do. That's why it's critical that you know exactly what content area—and standards—your activities are linked to.

Where to Learn More

- My book *Active Learning Across the Curriculum* offers hundreds of activities under the content areas of art, emergent literacy, math, music, science, and social studies. Another possibility is *The Kinesthetic Classroom* by Traci Lengel and Mike Kuczala.

- My book *Teachable Transitions* offers 190 activities to help children transition creatively from arrival to departure.

(Continued)

(Continued)

- "Make Transitions Trouble-Free & Teachable" is an online course for early childhood professionals. It offers many activities for the six typical daily transitions and can be found here:

  https://raepica.teachable.com/p/make-transitions-trouble-free-teachable/

- *Acting Out!: Avoid Behavior Challenges With Active Games & Activities* offers circle games for building community and includes a chapter on brain breaks. Eric Jensen's *Learning With the Body in Mind* also includes brain breaks (what he calls energizers) as well as rationale for them.

- My YouTube channel offers many videos on brain breaks, active learning, transitions, and more. You can find it here:

  https://www.youtube.com/channel/UC-d20r_dzRuJdQ7J0TEZOMQ

- Listen to "Fitting Fitness Into the Curriculum" here:

  https://www.bamradionetwork.com/track/fitting-fitness-into-the-curriculum/

PART III

Teaching With Children's Futures in Mind

CHAPTER 19

"What Is That?": How We Unwittingly Dampen Children's Creative Development

A young boy, whose teacher has assigned the class to draw horses, beams with pride at the blue horse he created. But his teacher returns the drawing with a grade of F, telling him that horses are either white, black, or brown. The boy is confused, however, because in his living room is a painting by Franz Marc, in which blue horses roam a brightly colored field.

A first-grade class is asked to draw butterflies like the one the teacher has drawn on the board. One girl happily decorates her butterfly with purple polka dots. But she's scolded because the teacher's butterfly doesn't have any polka dots.

A kindergarten student whose father, an artist, had once marveled at the child's ability to capture on paper the essence of a sailing scene, came home from school discouraged by her "failure" to properly create a sailboat. The teacher, it seems, required that sailboats be replicated from dittoed triangles.

These are three of many stories I've come across over the years. Another, more general, story came during a conversation with early childhood educator Amanda Morgan (see "Where to Learn More"), when she mentioned the number of teachers she's witnessed who "fix" the children's works so they're acceptable for posting, or for parents' approval.

Naturally, all of these teachers believe they're helping the children. Still, it's easy to see how their insistence upon perfection and "reality" can put a damper on the children's creativity and their future enthusiasm for creating. But even less obvious, more "innocent" comments we make when children present us with their imaginative offerings can be detrimental to creative development. Asking "What is that?" is one of them.

It's no surprise we're often stumped by the children's creations. Is it a dog? Is it a firehouse? Could it be a swamp creature? But the simple fact is that it doesn't matter what we see because we're looking at these handiworks from our point of view—from an *adult's* point of view—and it is the children's point of view that matters. If they want to tell us what they've produced, they will. But, often, it won't occur to them to inform us because it's not as important to them as is the enjoyment they feel in creating it.

When we ask children "What is that?" we are not-so-subtly letting them know that it has to *be* something. We are valuing product over process—just as the teachers in the examples above did. We are telling children that the joy and excitement they felt in the course of creating doesn't matter as much as our desire to see something we can identify.

Those who've been in my keynotes and trainings know that I'm a big fan of divergent problem solving—challenges to which there are multiple responses. I want to see it employed as much as possible, in as many content areas as possible, in early childhood settings because when children get into later grades, they unfortunately will see little of it. Indeed, they will be presented with worksheets and standardized tests in which there is only one "correct" answer. And they will come to believe that this is the way of the world. They will come to believe that "smart people" are the ones who always know that one right answer.

But people who think creatively are those who can imagine. That means they can imagine solutions to problems and challenges requiring more than one answer. They can imagine answers to the question, *What if?* And because they can imagine what it is like to be someone or something else, they can feel empathy—a quality as much in demand in the 21st century as any other real-world skill. So, it behooves us to *encourage* children's creative development wherever we see it—because creativity is about so much more than art!

The important adults in children's lives (you) have tremendous influence over their attitudes. They can either help or hinder creative development simply by paying careful attention to their words. Perhaps the teachers of Picasso and Kandinsky at one time asked, "What is that?" If so, these artists were among the lucky ones who shrugged it off and continued to paint what they saw in their minds. But we can't take that chance with the children in our care because the odds are far greater that if asked that question too often—or, worse, if they are the recipients of negative feedback—they will simply decide it's not worth it and give up any creative pursuits.

Albert Einstein famously said, "Imagination is more important than knowledge. For knowledge is limited, whereas imagination embraces the entire world, stimulating progress, giving birth to evolution." I'm inclined to believe he knew what he was talking about.

What's a Teacher to Do?

• Just as we tell children to watch their words, we have to be careful with our own. Below are examples of discouraging phrases, followed by those that are more encouraging:

• "There is no such thing as a blue horse" limits what is possible and dampens the children's ideas. If we say, "I see you made your horse blue!" we validate their choices.

(Continued)

(Continued)

- "I'll show you how to do it" focuses on the "right" way and discourages experimentation. But "You try it; I'm sure you can" encourages creative risk-taking.

- "That's not what pots and pans are for" limits possible uses for materials and makes children feel that new ideas are not acceptable. If we say, "You've made some musical instruments out of the pots and pans!" we're offering congratulations on the discovery.

- "What is that?" focuses on the product rather than the process. But describing what we see—"You used a lot of purple in your painting!"—encourages without judgment. And that's just the kind of encouragement children need for their creative development.

- Allow children to start projects from scratch. Often, teachers employ their own creativity in producing products—cutouts and such—that children are invited to add to. When all children start from the same point, inspiration and innovation are discouraged. Such is also the case when children are asked, for example, to draw turkeys from handprints.

- Proudly display children's creations *as is*, rather than doctoring them to meet with the approval of adults.

- Whenever possible—and necessary—explain the value of process over product to parents so the children will have complete freedom of expression at home also.

- Whenever possible, use divergent problem-solving across the curriculum, helping children to see that there's more than one way to meet a challenge (see the next chapter for more on this).

Where to Learn More

- Listen to "Valuing and Enjoying the Process of Learning," a 17-minute podcast featuring early childhood expert Amanda Morgan:

  http://www.bamradionetwork.com/student-centric-strategies/4487-valuing-and-enjoying-the-process-of-learning

- Listen to "Is It Possible That Creativity Is Misunderstood and Undervalued?" This is a 10-minute conversation with educator Stacey Goodman and James C. Kaufman, a professor of educational psychology:

  http://www.bamradionetwork.com/educators-channel/2300-is-it-possible-that-creativity-is-misunderstood-and-undervalued

- Written resources include MaryAnn Kohl's books, *Preschool Art: It's the Process, Not the Product* and *Primary Art: It's the Process, Not the Product*.

CHAPTER 20

Beyond "One Right Answer": How to Promote Children's Thinking Skills

How many things have changed since you arrived on the planet?

I don't even want to think about the number of changes I've witnessed over the course of my lifetime. But I can say one thing about them: They used to come more slowly! Over the past couple of decades, however, that has not been the case. The world is now changing so rapidly it seems that if we blink an eye, there's some new piece of technology to learn or some new problem in the world that needs fixing. And the more complex the world becomes, the more complex the problems.

The point is that, given the rate at which change is accelerating, we have no idea what the world will look like when today's four-year-olds are young professionals. The fact that we're still educating them in a school system that functions like it did 150 years ago is preposterous. For the most part, now that the internet exists, rote learning in general is a waste of time and energy.

Memorizing facts will have little use in life once a child has passed all the many tests schools require—unless the child intends to become a contestant on television game shows. And filling in bubbles? Don't get me started.

But the ability to meet challenges and solve problems? That will serve them no matter *what* the future looks like. We *know* this, but we still have them filling in bubbles. We're still training them to believe there's always going to be just one right answer to every question. It's ridiculous.

When children become convinced of the value of one right answer, what becomes of their critical- and creative-thinking skills? We may believe creativity is something necessary for artists only, but that's simply not the case. We need creativity in medicine if we're to find new healing methods. We need creativity in science if we're to discover answers to the world's mysteries.

We need creativity in business if we're to meet the challenges of a shrinking world. We need creativity in life if we're to find solutions to the trials we encounter.

If children become convinced of the value of one right answer, how will they ever trust in their ability to solve problems? Business leaders, in fact, are already finding themselves among such young people. One of their chief complaints about today's employees is their inability to think creatively.

So, how do we help children learn how to meet challenges? Well, active learning, of course, is the opposite of rote memorization. It's why I'm such a fierce proponent of it. The children are using their minds and bodies to explore and discover...and to *think* and create.

But there's one aspect of active learning that's essential if we're going to promote children's thinking skills, and that's divergent problem solving: the ability to respond in multiple ways to a single challenge.

Here are several examples:

- If you're working on geometry and you ask the children to show you a triangle with their body or body parts, some might use the whole body to demonstrate it, while others use just their arms, their legs, or their fingers.
- If you're exploring the science concept of balance and you've asked the children to demonstrate balance using

just two body parts, one child, who doesn't feel especially confident, might simply stand on his two feet. Another might balance on a hand and a foot. And still another—who may be enrolled in a gymnastics program—might balance on two knees. But there are also many other possibilities for balancing on two body parts: a knee and an elbow, a knee and the top of the head, or two cheeks!

- If you've asked the children to show you a crooked shape with their body or body parts, there can be as many different responses as there are children.
- A request to use manipulatives to demonstrate a quantity of *nine* can result in groupings of three threes, one and eight, or five and four, among others.
- Invite children to predict how a story will end, and they'll share many, many inventive possibilities with you.

Not only does divergent problem solving allow all children to respond at whatever level they're capable, offering plenty of opportunity for success; also, it helps children think outside the bubble—and to realize there isn't always going to be just "one right answer" to every question or problem. This inspires them to take greater creative risks. I've witnessed it!

Certainly, convergent thinking has its place in the world: Two plus two will always equal four, and the right combination of hydrogen and oxygen will always produce water. But we do real harm to our children—and the future of our world—if we convince them that convergent thinking is the only kind of thinking there is.

What's a Teacher to Do?

- Use the examples given as a jumping-off point for your own divergent-thinking challenges. While some topics lend themselves more freely to multiple responses, there are possibilities for its use within every content area.

(Continued)

(Continued)

• Note that, with any kind of problem solving, participants in the process will first come up with the most commonplace response. For example, if you're playing a game of cooperative musical chairs and you've asked the children to find a way to share the remaining chairs at the end of each round, their first likely response is to try to pile on top of one another. Your challenge is to encourage them to find another way, and then another and another. You can do so by acknowledging their initial response and then simply inviting them to show you a different way.

• To encourage divergent thinking, it's important to validate the different responses you receive. For example, if you ask the children to create a wide shape and you comment on Brady's high, wide shape, the children will rush to imitate Brady's response. But if you say something like, "I see Brady's in a high wide shape, Keisha is in a low wide shape, and Mia's wide shape is in between," the children will understand that responding in different ways is a good thing!

• Along those same lines, when implementing divergent problem solving, you should not demonstrate possible responses, as the children will merely imitate you.

• Your feedback should always be neutral; for example, "I see your three-point balance uses two hands and a foot," or "I see you're using your arms to show me a round shape!" Neutral feedback conveys the impression that there is no one right way.

Where to Learn More

- Educator John Spencer offers "7 Ways to Inspire Divergent Thinking in the Classroom":

  http://www.spencerauthor.com/divergent-thinking/

- This 13-minute podcast episode offers a lively panel discussion on "Teaching Creativity in a Climate That Discourages It":

  https://www.bamradionetwork.com/track/teaching-creativity-in-a-climate-that-discourages-it-2-2/

- The University of Texas at Austin offers a PDF titled "How to Teach: Divergent Thinking":

  https://facultyinnovate.utexas.edu/sites/default/files/TeachingGuide_HowtoTeachDivergentThinking.pdf

- Dr. Alice Sterling Honig has written "How to Promote Creative Thinking" with young children in mind:

  https://www.researchgate.net/publication/281408290_How_to_promote_creative_thinking

- Watch Sir Ken Robinson's excellent TED Talk, "Do Schools Kill Creativity?" here:

  https://www.youtube.com/watch?v=iG9CE55wbtY

CHAPTER 21

Should We Be Talking About Sexism in Early Childhood Education?

The short answer to the question posed in the title is *yes*. While it may seem as though the #MeToo and Time's Up movements have nothing to do with young children, the experts tell us that sexism does indeed begin in early childhood. In fact, psychology professor and author of *Parenting Beyond Pink and Blue*, Christia Spears Brown, told me in a BAM!radio podcast that sexism begins at birth! And when we consider the pink and blue phenomenon—and how differently girl babies are treated from boy babies, even prenatally—we have to admit that what she says makes sense.

Sexism begins with gender stereotyping, which is all too easy to reinforce. Christia and other experts contend that every time teachers say something like, "Good morning, boys and girls," attention is given to gender. And the more often statements like these are made ("Boys line up here, girls line up there." "What a good girl you're being."), the more children get the message that gender matters—a lot. And that's when they start making black-and-white generalizations about the meaning of gender.

Yes, I know; statements like these seem perfectly innocent. But what if they're not?

According to a *Slate* article on this topic, "The more ingrained kids' gender stereotypes become, the more easily they conclude that girls are inferior to boys—that boys have higher status because they biologically deserve it." Studies have also shown that "the more strongly boys believe these stereotypes, the more likely they are to make sexual comments, to tell sexual jokes in front of girls, and to grab women."

Those are statements that make me want to cry—especially considering that Christia told me 90 percent of girls in high school have been sexually harassed.

That's a stunning statistic, but perhaps one that shouldn't surprise me, considering how many #MeToo hashtags showed up among my own Facebook connections. And, of course, I posted the hashtag as well. When I was 19 years old, I was fired from a job for refusing to be "mauled" by the assistant manager, who seemed to believe it was his right to paw all of the young women in the office. He told the manager that my work was lacking, when nothing could have been further from the truth. But nobody asked me; the manager just took the man's word for it and I was let go.

Unfortunately, at the time no one used the phrase "sexual harassment" and there was certainly nowhere to turn for justice. So, I slunk home, and it wasn't long after that I decided working in the outside world wasn't right for me and I began working from home. It was lonely, but at least the only paws I encountered belonged to my cats!

"Hiding out" at home certainly won't be the solution for everyone, or even the majority of people who face gender discrimination. But if we begin to create change in early childhood, hiding out at home won't be necessary—because gender discrimination and stereotyping will become a thing of the past.

Christia assured me that small things can have a lasting impact. And I sure hope that's true because small things are easily done. But, of course, as with everything that matters, the hard part begins with our own awareness.

**What's a
Teacher to Do?**

• Christia and my other two guests on the podcast, educators Jill Berkowicz and Jason Flom, suggested that teachers embrace the power of gender neutrality in the classroom. Specifically, they advocated for removing gender from the language used (for example, "Boys will be boys."), making sure girls play in the block area and boys in the dress-up area, and ensuring that girls and boys play *together*. Quoted in the *Slate* article, child development expert Carol Martin says, "When they interact with each other like this, both girls and boys learn about each other and their similarities, become more comfortable with one another, and we believe that it may provide a kind of social resiliency allowing them to deal with a range of social experiences."

• If you hear a child say something like, "Girls can't do that," or "Only boys are allowed here"—well, talk about your teachable moment! You can either address it and ensure the kids get a lesson in gender equality, or you can let it slide. But the latter will teach them too. It will teach them that gender does indeed matter—and not in a good way.

• Be sure to talk to girls about more than their appearance. As I wrote in "Teaching Girls They're More Than a Pretty Face," in *What If Everybody Understood Child Development?*, girls are too often admired for their appearance only. That contributes to their own belief that they are "less than."

Where to Learn More

- To listen to the 10-minute discussion that inspired this chapter, click here:

  https://www.bamradionetwork.com/track/gender-stereo types-is-this-really-a-problem/

- Although written specifically for parents, I highly recommend you read the *Slate* article. You'll find it here:

  https://slate.com/human-interest/2017/11/how-to-stop-sexism-and-raise-a-son-who-respects-women.html

- Review the study, "Teaching Children to Confront Peers' Sexist Remarks: Implications for Theories of Gender Development and Educational Practice," here:

  https://link.springer.com/article/10.1007/s11199-009-9634-4

- In a 2010 study, researchers asked preschool teachers to emphasize gender in one classroom for two weeks, testing the children's attitudes about gender before and after. You can find the abstract here:

  https://www.ncbi.nlm.nih.gov/pubmed/21077864

CHAPTER 22

"Be Careful!": Teaching Children to Fear

How many times do you imagine a child hears an adult say, "Be careful!"? I suspect it's a close second to them hearing, "No!" And, if it's a female child, it may be the number-one phrase coming at them, as girls tend to be cautioned far more often than boys. One study determined that girls are told to be careful four times more often than boys!

This phrase, of course, is a clear and persistent message that one shouldn't take too many risks. That there are far too many hazards in the world. So, children learn to "stay safe." They learn to fear.

But outright cautions aren't the only way in which children are receiving those messages. When a school takes away all traditional playground equipment and replaces it with safe, sanitized (read: *boring*) plastic, they don't need to hear the concern spoken aloud to get the message.

When children aren't allowed to walk—or do much of anything, really—alone, the not-so-subliminal message is that they need to be protected...from *everything*. When a school bans tag or cartwheels, children learn that it's safer to be sedentary than physically active. An online search for the term "school bans cartwheels" brings up 638,000 results from the United States to

Canada to Australia. A search on "school bans tag" results in 86,800,000 listings. That tells me we've got a real problem.

Our society—and its 24-hour news cycles—have generated so much fear that if parents and educators could literally bubble-wrap kids, I believe they would. But, as Lenore Skenazy of the Free-Range Kids movement repeatedly points out, we're prioritizing fear over facts! This was evident to me when I read that yet another school had banned cartwheels on the playground—not because there had been any injuries from cartwheels, but because the *potential* for injuries existed. Does that mean we should no longer let children ride in cars, or walk down stairs?

Yes, we want to protect our children. But decisions like these often signify that the adults involved are placing their needs above those of the kids. Because, the fact is, children need to take risks. Indeed, they were created to do so—and to know just how far they can push the boundaries. As research professor and play advocate Dr. Peter Gray points out, risky play teaches children emotional resilience. We believe we're protecting children when we bubble-wrap them, but the truth is that children who grow up afraid of risk will not be resilient. They will not be problem-solvers. They will certainly not be able to handle risk, which is inherent in life, when it comes along. Often, they will crumble when faced with challenge. Just ask any college counselor about the unprecedented number of visits they receive from students these days for the most minor of issues. Ask the authors of *The Coddling of the American Mind*, who offer plenty of evidence that overprotection does more harm than good.

We wouldn't keep a child from learning to speak, or read, and then expect them to suddenly know how to do so as an adult. Why is it we think we can keep children from learning to take risks—from learning to overcome challenges—and that they'll miraculously acquire the ability later in life simply because they've grown taller?

In a 2017 article, associate professor of pediatrics Mariana Brussoni writes,

> ...it's not up to parents or experts to decide what is risky play for a particular child. Rather, children need to be given the mental and physical space to figure out the appropriate risk levels for themselves: far enough that it feels exhilarating, but not so far that it becomes too scary.

It may seem to be a kindness when we issue cautionary messages. But if we allow children to take reasonable risks and to explore their capabilities and limitations, then we'll know we've truly protected and prepared them for what lies ahead.

What's a Teacher to Do?

• On Facebook, the Child and Nature Alliance of Canada posted a helpful chart offering alternatives to "Be careful." They included possibilities such as

- "What's your next move?"
- "Do you feel safe there?"
- "Stay focused on what you're doing."
- "What's your plan with that big stick?" (That's my personal favorite.)

• Conviction is essential if you're going to convince parents, administrators, and even yourself that risky play is worth the risk. Use the resources below to build your argument and become an advocate.

• Like saying "Good job!," saying "Be careful!" is often habitual. But practice makes perfect. If you can first hear the words in your head and take a deep breath before issuing a cautionary message, eventually *not* issuing one will become habit.

Where to Learn More

- I highly recommend *The Coddling of the American Mind: How Good Intentions and Bad Ideas Are Setting Up a Generation for Failure*, by Greg Lukianoff and Jonathan Haidt.

(Continued)

(Continued)

- Read Dr. Peter Gray's "Risky Play: Why Children Love It and Need It":

  https://www.psychologytoday.com/us/blog/freedom-learn/201404/risky-play-why-children-love-it-and-need-it

- Dr. Mariana Brussoni offers "Why Kids Need Risk, Fear and Excitement in Play":

  http://theconversation.com/why-kids-need-risk-fear-and-excitement-in-play-81450

- Listen to "Risky Child's Play: The Good, the Bad, and the Mostly Good" on BAM!radio:

  https://www.bamradionetwork.com/track/risky-child-play-the-good-the-bad-and-the-ugly/

- Read "The Overprotected Kid" here:

  https://www.theatlantic.com/magazine/archive/2014/04/hey-parents-leave-those-kids-alone/358631/

- The *Journal of Applied Developmental Psychology* published a study called "Parental Influences on Toddlers' Injury-Risk Behaviors: Are Sons and Daughters Socialized Differently?" You can find the abstract here:

  https://www.sciencedirect.com/science/article/pii/S0193397399000155

- Caroline Paul's "Why Do We Teach Girls That It's Cute to Be Scared?" is a good read and includes studies that have demonstrated girls are cautioned more often than boys. You can read it here:

  https://www.nytimes.com/2016/02/21/opinion/sunday/why-do-we-teach-girls-that-its-cute-to-be-scared.html

- Information about a study titled "What Is the Relationship Between Risky Outdoor Play and Health in Children? A Systematic Review" can be found here:

  https://www.mdpi.com/1660-4601/12/6/6423

CHAPTER 23

School Shootings: What Does Early Childhood Have to Do With Them?

School shootings aren't the kind of thing I typically write about—because the topic would certainly seem to have nothing to do with early childhood. But I've been thinking a lot about school shootings and have found myself asking: What *is* it that incites such rage in these young people that they see *killing* as the only resort?

Immediately following all of these horrible incidents, everybody talks about the need for more attention to mental health, in addition to gun control. I absolutely agree that both are essential. But if you're like me, you probably first think about mental health as it relates to people old enough to purchase or acquire guns. People who have been bullied or ignored for so long that something finally snaps in them.

Upon reflection, however, I've realized we can probably assume that the kind of anger, frustration, and helplessness—the mental health issues—evident in school shooters doesn't just suddenly crop up. It *builds*! And based on what I know to be happening in the education and lives of today's young children, I've become convinced that it often does begin in early childhood.

Let's think about it. According to a 2013 article, depression affects approximately 4 percent of preschoolers in the United States today, with the number diagnosed increasing by *23 percent every year*. And the Citizens Commission on Human Rights offers disturbing information relative to the number of children taking psychiatric drugs in this country.

Why are so many preschoolers depressed and on psychiatric drugs? Yes, there are those whose conditions are inherited from parents. But I also read and hear enough stories from parents and early childhood professionals to know that we as a society make an awful lot of little ones awfully unhappy. And why *shouldn't* they be unhappy?

- We take away their play. During a BAM!radio interview, early childhood expert Nancy Carlsson-Paige asked, if we don't allow children to express their feelings through play, as nature intended, where do those feelings go?
- As I've previously indicated, we demand that young children accomplish things for which they are in no way developmentally equipped. Ready or not, we want them to read by the end of kindergarten. Ready or not, we expect them to play like Beckham before they're barely past the wobbling stage. Adult expectations create a ridiculous amount of pressure for a little one.
- Despite knowing that physical activity reduces stress, we remove nearly all opportunities for physical activity from their lives.
- We pit them against one another, at earlier and earlier ages, with our focus on competition and winning, despite the fact that competition promotes antisocial behaviors.
- When we unnecessarily overprotect them, making them afraid of *everything*, as discussed in the previous chapter, we take away children's security and sense of control.

And, in addition to all of that, we stifle their natural creativity, offer them no downtime, keep them from the outdoor light they require, and stifle their social–emotional development with virtual experiences, all of which I've addressed in previous chapters.

Given all of this, imagine how the children feel. Imagine the frustration and helplessness building as their freedoms are taken from them, including the freedom to just be children. As they are given so little *choice*. As they become more and more disconnected from the real world and the people in it.

Some will snap. Not all of them, certainly, and not even the majority. But those who do will have, in one way or another, lost their lives. Lost the promise and potential with which they were born. And they will have cost the lives of numerous others.

So, yes, unfortunately, this *is* a chapter about both school shootings and early childhood. I fear that until we stop treating young children like small adults—until we start allowing them to experience childhood as it was meant to be experienced—we will see this kind of rage over and over and over again.

What's a Teacher to Do?

• We have to do more than wring our hands and weep copious tears when we hear of school shootings. Each of us has to keep fighting the good fight. Parents only want the best for their children, but thanks to all the misinformation they receive, they don't always know what that is. Policymakers don't always know—or seem to care—about the research concerning what's best for children. That's why each of us has to do our part to educate both groups. Each of us has to do whatever we can to create change so that our children have far less reason to feel angry, frustrated, and helpless!

• If you're in a setting that implements developmentally inappropriate practices, use the research and the suggestions in the next section of this book to educate decision-makers.

• If necessary, be subversive! I know it's difficult to go against the grain when your job is on the line, but we have to put the children's needs first. If you have to sneak play and developmentally appropriate practices into your

(Continued)

(Continued)

setting, sneak them in! If you're forced to implement developmentally inappropriate practice, such as doing worksheets, do whatever you can to make it as painless as possible for the children. Add as much love as you can to the process. Love goes a long way with the little ones.

• Advocate for a mental health professional in your school or center. If having one is impossible and the need seems urgent, reach out to one for advice on your own.

• Reduce screen time, which produces anxiety and depression in some children. The children in your care are likely getting plenty (i.e., too much) screen time at home. Yours can be a screen-free environment that focuses on relationships.

• Get the children outdoors as often as possible! Nature is a powerful antidote to anxiety and frustration.

• Focus on cooperative, as opposed to competitive, practices. Among other things, that means doing away with rewards such as gold stars and such shaming practices as behavior charts.

Where to Learn More

• "Number of Children & Adolescents Taking Psychiatric Drugs in the U.S.":

https://www.cchrint.org/psychiatric-drugs/children-on-psychiatric-drugs/

• Read "Not Just a Phase: Depression in Preschoolers" here:

https://www.psychologytoday.com/us/blog/talking-about-trauma/201306/not-just-phase-depression-in-preschoolers

- Harvard's Center on the Developing Child offers an overview of early childhood mental health here:

  https://developingchild.harvard.edu/science/deep-dives/mental-health/

- Learn about the study "Associations Between Screen Time and Lower Psychological Well-Being Among Children and Adolescents: Evidence From a Population-Based Study" here:

  https://www.sciencedirect.com/science/article/pii/S221133 5518301827

- For information on the above-mentioned study, as well as other information regarding the subject, read *Time*'s piece, "There's Worrying New Research About Kids' Screen Time and Their Mental Health":

  https://time.com/5437607/smartphones-teens-mental-health/

CHAPTER 24

Life Lessons Learned From Lunchtime

Many years ago, I consulted in an elementary school in Maine. When the PE teacher said he preferred having lunch in the cafeteria, as opposed to the teachers' lounge, I decided to join him. It had been a while since I'd dined in a school cafeteria, and I wanted to relive it. But what I experienced in that cafeteria was nothing like what I recalled from my own school days.

In my time, lunch wasn't just about eating but also about socializing. Except for recess it was the one chance during the school day to talk with friends, exchanging thoughts and sharing information about the events in our lives. I'm sure we also picked up a life lesson or two about manners and etiquette; for example, if we talked with our mouths full no one could understand what we were saying. But mostly we learned important lessons in communication. After all, one learns to communicate by communicating.

However, in that Maine elementary school there was no talking allowed during lunch. The students were there to eat—and to eat only—and there were teachers stationed strategically throughout the cafeteria to ensure the rule wasn't broken.

Unfortunately, these adults brought to mind Gestapo standing guard.

At the time—and for a number of years—I believed this school's policy was an exception. An aberration. But I've since learned that there are many, many schools where the no-talking rule is enforced. Moreover, with recess now limited to a few scant minutes during the day (if offered at all)—and too often following lunch instead of preceding it, as it should—lunchtime is typically a rushed and stressful event.

An email from a distraught mom confirmed this. After just a few days in kindergarten, she wrote, her son, "Sam," was already anxious and stressed—due to lunch!

On Sam's *first day of kindergarten*, he was confronted with the ugly truth that school isn't necessarily a friendly place. As he reported to his mom, "I opened my lunch and I just got started, and you know what the lady did? She just shut my lunch box and said 'zip it up.' I just got started!"

Apparently, Sam and his classmates had only 20 minutes for lunch and 15 minutes for recess, down five minutes from the previous school year. This didn't give him enough time to eat everything his parents packed for him. By day three Sam was enormously upset and pleading with his mother not to give him a whole sandwich, which would take too long to consume, or a juice pouch, which would take too long to open.

His mother tried to explain that she wanted to give him options and he wasn't required to eat everything. To which he replied, "MOM, you don't understand; I won't have time!" He protested that even if able to eat a whole sandwich he wouldn't have time to eat anything else and it would just be wasted— something he couldn't tolerate.

How sad! I have to ask: Should a five-year-old get less time to eat than the average adult worker? Should a five-year-old be experiencing such high levels of stress? If the intention is to increase cortisol levels in children and make them detest school right from the get-go, then this school gets an A+.

Perhaps it's too much to ask that everyone understand child development. Perhaps it's even too much to ask that everybody *working with kids* understand it. But is it too much to ask that everyone working with them show them some respect? Maybe even a little kindness or empathy?

Do the people who decide to schedule 20-minute, no-talking lunch periods for small children take the children into consideration *at all*?

Sam's mom, who is an early childhood professional, told me that she shared her concern (and rage) with her co-teacher. Her colleague's response was that she should become a kindergarten teacher in order to know how it really is on the front lines. In other words, she was another adult who didn't take the children into consideration.

The only life lessons children learn in these situations are that (1) communication/socializing is not a good thing; (2) meals are not meant to be enjoyed; and (3) life is hard! And, of course, (4) school stinks.

Is this what we want young children to glean from their education? The whole notion of rushed, no-talking lunch periods infuriates me. I mean, despite the fact that they're both institutions, schools are *not* supposed to resemble prisons.

What's a Teacher to Do?

• It's been shown that recess before lunch decreases food waste and improves student behavior. If your school offers recess after lunch, use the information on the next page and more (there's plenty out there) to try to have the policy changed.

• Share the research from Harvard University (below) with decision-makers, who need to understand that kids don't have enough time to eat lunch.

• If your school has silent and/or rushed lunch periods, invite parents and policymakers to join the kids for lunch one day. Let them experience what it's like!

Where to Learn More

- Watch this video of a lunch period in an elementary school in Japan, and if you're so inclined, jot down the number of life lessons learned here. I can assure you that your list will be long—and that everything on it will serve these students well, both in the present and in the future. You'll find it here:

  https://www.youtube.com/watch?v=hL5mKE4e4uU

- The National Education Association addresses "Recess Before Lunch" here:

  http://www.nea.org/archive/43158.htm

- Peaceful Playgrounds offers a PDF titled "Benefits of Recess Before Lunch," which includes, in addition to the benefits, solutions to concerns and research citations. You'll find it here:

  https://www.peacefulplaygrounds.com/download/lunch/benefits-recess-before-lunch-facts.pdf

- Read this piece titled "Elementary School Students Forced to Eat Lunch in Complete Silence":

  https://www.sheknows.com/parenting/articles/1114267/texas-kids-forced-to-eat-lunch-in-silence/

- Action for Healthy Kids' "Time to Eat" offers steps you can take to advocate for longer lunch periods:

  https://www.actionforhealthykids.org/activity/time-to-eat/

- Read about a recent Harvard University study that determined kids don't get enough time to eat lunch here:

  https://philadelphia.cbslocal.com/2019/10/08/study-students-arent-getting-enough-time-to-eat-lunch/

CHAPTER 25

Children Are Losing Their Connection to Nature and the Consequences Are Real

Did you happen to see the Nature Valley ad from a couple of years ago, in which they sit down with three generations of families and ask, "What did you like to do for fun as a kid?"

The two older generations, of course, had answers that involved the outdoors and nature: tobogganing, picking blueberries, building forts. Then, unfortunately, as I'm sure you can imagine, the youngest generation responded with some version of "Play video games" or "Watch videos." That was upsetting enough, but what really turned my stomach was the amount of time they spent doing it, and their dependency on it.

It's been over 14 years since I first read Richard Louv's *Last Child in the Woods: Saving Our Children From Nature-Deficit Disorder*. I remember how appalled I was when I read the response of a six-year-old asked if he preferred the indoors or the outdoors. He said he favored the indoors because that's where the plugs are. I couldn't conceive of any six-year-old child—least of all a boy child—not wanting to be outside! Yet, all these years later, things have only gotten worse. Not one of the children in the Nature Valley ad preferred outdoor activities, choosing instead to sit for hours at a time with eyes glued to a screen offering *virtual* activities.

Even if we fail to consider all of the potential physical and mental health problems that can arise from too much screen time, we can't overlook the consequences of children losing their connection to nature.

Reports indicate that fewer than 10 percent of US children currently learn about nature from being outside. Instead, one-third of them learn about it at school and, believe it or not, more than half of them learn about it via such electronic devices as computers and television. A tweeted photo of kindergartners sitting at a computer, with the caption, "Students learning about habitats," was certainly an example of that.

Surely we can agree that books and electronics offer no substitute for the real thing. Being outdoors is an experience of the senses, which is how much of young children's learning takes place. Outside there are myriad amazing things to see: creatures in the clouds, hummingbirds hovering, ants at work, and four-leaf clovers. To hear: birdsong, leaves rustling in the breeze, brooks babbling. To smell: lilacs, rain-soaked ground, and Concord grapes. To touch: the velvety softness of a petal, a fallen feather, the bark of a tree, or mud puddles. There are even things to taste, like newly fallen snow or a freshly picked blueberry. And if you recall from your own childhood, even the simplest foods taste better outside. Somehow, a peanut butter sandwich is just a sandwich when it's eaten in a kitchen, but make it part of a picnic and suddenly it's special.

Richard Louv coined the phrase "nature-deficit disorder" because he maintains that as children spend less and less of their lives in natural surroundings, "their senses narrow, physiologically and psychologically, and this reduces the richness of human experience."

Indeed, to be human is to be part of nature. We evolved in the outdoors! And as much as we may have changed since our days as cave dwellers, our brains are still hardwired for an existence in nature. We therefore have an innate link with it that, when broken, leaves a part of us bereft.

Moreover, nature plays a major role in our aesthetic sense. Ecologist Stephen R. Kellert writes that the development of this sense is "instrumental in a child's emerging capacity for perceiving and recognizing order and organization, for developing ideas of harmony, balance, and symmetry." This is in addition to the primary benefit of our aesthetic sense: the heightening of our awareness of beauty.

As Richard Louv writes: "When we deny our children nature, we deny them beauty."

Finally, when we keep children indoors, we convey the message that the outdoor environment is of little significance. How, then, are children to learn to care for the environment? Why would they work to preserve something that they've been taught to disregard, or for which they have so little feeling? Considering our environment is all we have to live in (until scientists find a way for us to live on the moon), it's to everyone's advantage if our children learn to love and value it while they're young. And that requires having firsthand experience of it.

I understand that adults can be afraid of the outdoors. I can even understand why. But we need to get our priorities in order. The fear that keeps kids indoors is usually based on false information. What's happening to children as they lose their connection to nature is real. And we have some very real reasons to be frightened of those consequences.

What's a Teacher to Do?

- When studying something like habitats, use technology only as a *supplement* to what the children discover outdoors. Even creating habitats indoors is preferable to learning about them on a computer.

(Continued)

(Continued)

• The most obvious solution is to take the children outdoors as often as possible. You can even take activities like story time or art projects, typically associated with the indoors, outside. And what better place to experience science lessons? Why not invite the children, armed with paintbrushes and buckets of water, to "paint" the outside of the building in order to learn about absorption and evaporation?

• If you don't have access to trees and other "pretty" things we associate with nature, remember that insects and rocks are also part of nature.

• Encourage outdoor games that call attention to elements of nature. For example, in Touch It! the children each begin in their own personal space, the location of which they must remember. You then call out something such as, "Touch something smooth!" or "Touch something rough!" or "Touch something green!" The children run to touch something matching the description and then return to their personal space before you call out another challenge.

• If you're in an urban setting, ensure that the children have opportunities to look out the windows, searching for whatever elements of nature might be visible. Use the NAEYC resource on the next page for additional ideas.

Where to Learn More

• I strongly recommend Richard Louv's book, the full title of which is *Last Child in the Woods: Saving Our Children From Nature-Deficit Disorder*. I believe it's a must-read for everybody who cares about children.

- For a deeper dive, you might choose *Children in Nature: Psychological, Sociocultural, and Evolutionary Investigations*, edited by Peter H. Kahn Jr. and Stephen R. Kellert.

- For information on the impact of nature on health, check out the study, "Measuring Connectedness to Nature in Preschool Children in an Urban Setting and Its Relation to Psychological Functioning":

  https://journals.plos.org/plosone/article?id=10.1371/journal.pone.0207057

- For information on the impact of nature on cognitive functioning, you can access a PDF of Nancy M. Well's study, "At Home With Nature: Effects of 'Greenness' on Children's Cognitive Functioning" here:

  https://www.nrs.fs.fed.us/pubs/jrnl/2000/nc_2000_wells_001.pdf

- A PDF of "Coping With ADD: The Surprising Connection to Green Play Settings" can be accessed here:

  http://www.attitudematters.org/documents/Coping%20with%20ADD%20-%20Green%20Play%20Settings.pdf

- Listen to "What Is Nature Deficit? Why It Matters" here:

  https://www.bamradionetwork.com/track/what-is-nature-deficit-why-it-matters/

- NAEYC offers an article titled "From Puddles to Pigeons: Learning About Nature in Cities" for those in urban settings. Access it here:

  https://www.naeyc.org/resources/pubs/yc/nov2018/learning-about-nature-cities

PART IV

Advocacy

CHAPTER 26

Who Are We Protecting When We Ban Children's Activities?

Ask my oldest friend Sheila about our childhood, classes we took, or teachers we had, and she can rattle off information as though our childhood happened a week, not decades, ago. Me, not so much. I'm not sure why, but I remember very little—usually in snippets—about when I was a kid.

There are a few memories, however, that have stayed with me and remain strong all these years later. One is of mounting the front steps of my house and then climbing to the flat cement ledge alongside the top step. From there I jumped to the small, concrete, walled-in area below. It was a long and scary jump. It was terrifying, in fact, and if I thought about it too long, I'd back down. So, I climbed and jumped quickly!

I'm sure my knees are currently paying the price for the many times I leaped from that ledge. Still, I have no regrets about participating in this daredevil act, precisely because it *was* a daredevil act. It reminds me of the kind of kid I was. Of the kind of bravery I possessed. Of the risks I was willing to take. Perhaps it's true of all of us, but it seems I got less brave as the years went on. And when I do take a risk—one of the biggest being my move from New Hampshire to the DC area on my own—I hear myself telling people, "I can't believe I did that; it's not like me at all." But it *is* like the kid I was! So now when I find myself afraid of taking a risk, or of a new situation, I know I need to bring that kid to mind and recognize she's still inside of me.

Another memory is of an older neighborhood girl teaching me how to do a cartwheel. It didn't come easily, and I recall practicing it for days—over and over again down the middle of our street, until I finally got it right. What a glorious feeling of accomplishment that was. I demonstrated my cartwheels to everybody who'd watch!

That particular memory reminds me of just how persistent I can be—and that persistence does pay off.

So, it was with great sadness—and enormous frustration— that I read a piece titled "Banning Cartwheels: What's the Point of Recess With No Fun?"

According to the piece:

> *The cartwheel, not generally considered a thing of peril, has been banned, together with the entire family of activities it belongs to, commonly known as gymnastics. The powers that be have determined that these risky contortions of young bodies and outright defiance of the laws of gravity have no place on the school playground.*

Apparently, the staff at this particular elementary school was uncomfortable with the "level of risk"—this despite the fact that no child had ever been hurt performing gymnastics during recess.

Sadly, this school is only one of many taking similar actions. And I can't help but ask myself whether the adults in these instances are putting their needs ahead of the kids'. They may tell themselves they're protecting the children, but aren't they really just protecting themselves—from worry, from effort, and from the possibility of a lawsuit?

To my way of thinking, what they're costing the kids is beyond measure—because today's overprotected kids (no cartwheels, no sledding, no tag) will never have memories like the ones I've shared here. When daunted by the challenges of adulthood, they won't be able to look back and remember their courage and persistence in the face of formidable tasks and draw on the strength such memories could provide. And that's not just unfair and unfortunate; to me, it's a heck of a lot scarier to contemplate than a leap from any ledge could ever be.

What's a Teacher to Do?

• Weigh in on decisions regarding what comprises risky play. Is your school considering removing the monkey bars or banning tag? Bring information on the importance of risk-taking to the attention of decision-makers.

• Whenever you have the opportunity, encourage parents and administrators to remember their own childhoods! Didn't they have experiences that today would be considered risky? Didn't those experiences build character? Why wouldn't they want children to have similar experiences? What makes them riskier today?

• You may be a child's last chance to explore risky play. If your school has removed the possibility of risk, sneak it in wherever you can! For example, bring loose parts to the playground. Or place a jump rope on the ground and invite children to travel across it as though they were tightrope walkers.

• If you've created rules that prevent children from going up a slide or playing with sticks, for example, reflect on the reasons why. Is it for your own comfort level? What if you helped children understand personal space and instead of banning stick play, you implemented a rule about playing with them only within their own personal space?

• Make it a practice to get past "worst-first thinking." Instead of considering all the things that could possibly go wrong when children balance on a stump or go up a slide, contemplate all of the positive elements of these activities.

(Continued)

(Continued)

• When you observe a child doing something you consider risky, before stopping it, ask yourself if the risk is worth the reward.

Where to Learn More

• Listen to "Risky Child's Play: The Good, the Bad, and the Mostly Good" on BAM!radio:

https://www.bamradionetwork.com/track/risky-child-play-the-good-the-bad-and-the-ugly/

• You might also listen to "Are We Taking Playground Safety Too Far?":

https://www.bamradionetwork.com/track/are-we-taking-playground-safety-too-far-2/

• Dr. Peter Gray weighs in on "Risky Play: Why Children Love It and Need It":

https://www.psychologytoday.com/us/blog/freedom-learn/201404/risky-play-why-children-love-it-and-need-it

• Pediatric occupational therapist Angela Hanscom's book, *Balanced and Barefoot*, addresses risky play. You can read an excerpt here:

https://www.washingtonpost.com/news/answer-sheet/wp/2016/07/04/why-some-risky-play-is-necessary-for-kids/

• "How to Facilitate Risky Play in the Classroom" is a helpful article. You'll find it here:

https://blog.himama.com/how-to-facilitate-risky-play/

CHAPTER 27

The Real Dangers of Childhood: How Do We Help People See Them?

I'm not a fan of fear tactics. In fact, I often can be heard railing against them, as I believe the media's obsession with them has made adults—especially parents—paranoid, and has forced children into a childhood that doesn't look remotely like childhood *should*.

Take, for example, the belief that earlier is better. Whether we're discussing athletics or academics, parents fear that if they don't get their children involved in as much as possible, as soon as possible, their little ones will fall behind and never live up to their full potential. Thanks to this fear, far too many children are being asked to do that for which they're not developmentally ready. The result, as I've written, is frustration and failure for kids, and even an intense dislike for whatever it is they're asked to master—like reading and physical activity!

Another myth under which today's adults are laboring is that it is a dangerous, dangerous world and they must be ever-vigilant to prevent their children from being snatched, or worse. And why wouldn't they believe such a thing, when the evidence seems irrefutable? Whether it's via traditional or social media, we receive constant messages about child abduction and stranger danger. But the fact remains that stranger danger is yet another falsehood and children today are *no less safe* than they were when I was a kid (which was a very long time ago). But how are parents to know that? How are they to believe that when our society has become so adept at instilling fear?

In a recent Facebook discussion, the topic at hand was the age at which it's okay to let a child walk to school alone (junior high, said one, but only because she was watching from a hill). The general mindset of the discussion can be summed up in the comment of another woman, who wrote, "It's definitely dangerous to leave kids by themselves ever."

Ever?

In my naivete, I attempted to soothe the participants' fears. I shared the statistics showing that it's the safest time to be a kid in America, and the fact that even the Center for Missing and Exploited Children confirms stranger danger is a myth. The response I got? "Sex trafficking is real. Kidnapping, rape, and murder are real. I don't live in fear, I live in reality!"

Yes, they're "real." They've always *been* real, but it never before stopped adults from allowing children to be children. The difference between then and now is that potential danger is all anybody talks about now. And these potential dangers have become so exaggerated that our grasp on reality has become seriously skewed.

One of the consequences of the danger-lurks myth is that children aren't being allowed to take the risks that were once a natural part of childhood and of *growth*. Autonomy and the ability to problem-solve are among the characteristics being sacrificed at the altar of overprotection.

That's something adults truly *should* be afraid of. And here's another: that children will grow up scared and anxious. It simply doesn't make for strong, independent humans. In fact, this is already happening. The introduction to an article in *Psychology Today*, titled "A Nation of Wimps," states, "parental hyper-concern has the net effect of making kids more fragile; that may be why they're breaking down in record numbers."

In that article, social historian Peter Stearns is quoted as saying that parents have exaggerated many of the dangers of childhood while overlooking others, such as the demise of recess.

I couldn't agree more! Here are a few other issues more worthy of our concern:

- Children's sedentary lifestyles: With 40 percent of children ages five to eight years old showing at least one heart disease risk factor, including obesity and hypertension, and the first signs of arteriosclerosis appearing at age 6, adults should be *terrified* of letting children be inactive.
- Too much screen time: With a growing body of research showing that it causes vision problems, aggression, depression, and more, this is an issue that *must* be taken seriously.
- The elimination of free play from children's lives—for more reasons than I could list in one chapter.
- Children's lack of downtime, discussed in Chapter 9.

And this is just a partial list of the serious risks facing today's children. Sadly, they don't get the kind of press that crimes do. They don't get the airtime (fear-mongering sells, and money motivates)—or even the conversation—that potential hazards do.

So, I'm at a loss. If *statistics* aren't evidence enough, how are we to turn around this culture of fear? How can we allay parents'—and teachers' and administrators' and policy-makers'—misplaced angst? It's absolutely imperative that we do—because there truly is much to fear if we don't.

What's a Teacher to Do?

- When someone is making decisions about children based on a myth, we can't be afraid to correct them. Use data and the research to contradict false beliefs. It may seem impossible to change people's minds, but we can't give up trying.

- It may occasionally be necessary to use fear tactics ourselves. For example, when I share frightening information about the state of our children's health, I know my motivation is pure, unlike that of the media and marketers.

(Continued)

(Continued)

I remind myself that parents don't have the time to keep up with research and that, if I'm aware of it, I have a responsibility to share it.

• Do your best not to succumb to "worst-first thinking" yourself. If you're not certain something is true, look into it!

Where to Learn More

• You can find the article "A Nation of Wimps" here: https://www.psychologytoday.com/us/articles/200411/nation-wimps

• Read "There's Never Been a Safer Time to Be a Kid in America":
https://www.washingtonpost.com/news/wonk/wp/2015/04/14/theres-never-been-a-safer-time-to-be-a-kid-in-america/

• To quell fears regarding stranger danger, read "Five Myths About Missing Children":
https://www.washingtonpost.com/opinions/five-myths-about-missing-children/2013/05/10/efee398c-b8b4-11e2-aa9e-a02b765ff0ea_story.html

• Follow Let Grow (https://letgrow.org/) for myth-busting information.

• Read Frank Furedi's *How Fear Works* or Daniel Gardner's *The Science of Fear* for a better understanding of fear's contagion.

- Other pertinent books include *A Nation of Wimps* by Hara Estroff Marano and *Free-Range Kids: How to Raise Safe, Self-Reliant Children (Without Going Nuts With Worry)* by Lenore Skenazy. All of these books are not only worth reading, but worth recommending to parents and decision-makers.

CHAPTER 28

Shouldn't School Safety Drills Be Implemented With the Children in Mind?

As I've written previously, it's actually the safest time to be a kid in America. But hardly anybody believes that, and I get it. It's hard to believe.

It's hard to believe because we've had several horrific school shootings. It's hard to believe because we're inundated 24/7 with news, much of which is fear inducing. It's hard to believe because we've become so accustomed to worst-first thinking that we're no longer thinking straight. We're doing everything from banning physical play, to punishing parents who let their children go outside alone, to implementing school safety drills that can do more to terrify children than keep them safe. And we're doing it all in the name of prevention.

I do understand the intention behind school safety drills. They're intended to keep kids and teachers safe through preparation for potential harm. But, as with all decisions concerning children, shouldn't we keep the *children* in mind? Shouldn't school safety drills take into consideration the children's developmental levels and weigh the consequences of frightening them to the point of traumatizing them?

When I read Launa Hall's piece, "Rehearsing for Death: A PreK Teacher on the Trouble With Lockdown Drills," in *The Washington Post*, I was chilled. Then I took part in a #kinderchat on Twitter during which teachers mentioned just how many drills, of varying kinds, they have to do every year—and I was stunned.

Launa, a teacher in Arlington, Virginia, who at the time was teaching four- and five-year-olds, wrote about the challenges of explaining and executing a lockdown drill with preschoolers. Her choice of words had to be precise; for example, *activity* instead of *game*, because games are synonymous with laughter. She couldn't use the word *police* because some young children are afraid of police officers. She couldn't encourage them to be quiet because, being four and five years old, they would inevitably shush one another.

The drill Launa describes in her piece surely wasn't created with the needs of children in mind. With the *feelings* of the children in mind. And hers was a drill that only involved locking the classroom door and hiding in the closet. In other schools, there have been drills involving staged killings and fake blood. Drills that traumatize children nearly as much as an actual shooting can.

In another piece in *The Washington Post*, this one titled, "Lockdown Drills: An American Quirk, Out of Control," author Sergio Pecanha offers these headlines from schools around the country:

> *In Indiana, officials played a segment of a 911 call of a teacher in a panic during the Columbine High School shooting to students. In Ohio, officers fired blank shots during an active-shooter drill. In South Carolina, an officer dressed in black posed as an intruder on an unannounced drill. In Michigan, a school is spending $48 million on a renovation that includes curved hallways and hiding niches, in hopes of protecting students from a mass shooting. In Florida, a police officer arrested two 6-year-old students for misdemeanor battery. In Colorado, teachers received buckets and kitty litter for students to use as toilets in case of a prolonged school lockdown.*

He also relates the story of one school that adapted a lullaby to prepare kindergartners.

While a cute piggyback song will certainly appeal to young children, the lyrics in this case are more liable to induce fear. And for what purpose? Pecanha outlines some of the other ways in which children are more likely to die, none of which create panic and cause us to terrify kids.

When I was in school, we had fire drills. We lined up single-file and exited the classroom and the building. Administrators did *not* set fires throughout the school, and firefighters did not rush in, hoses blasting, so that we might be more fully prepared should the real thing happen. The idea of frightening children in that manner would have been considered preposterous back then. It should still be considered preposterous.

Pecanha concludes his piece with these words:

Misguided safety measures, such as dramatized lockdown drills, may give us the impression that we are protecting children, when, in fact, we are handing them a burden that adults are failing to address.

Hall concludes hers with these:

Instead of controlling guns and inconveniencing those who would use them, we are rounding up and silencing a generation of schoolchildren, and terrifying those who care for them. We are giving away precious time to teach and learn while we cower in fear.

What's a Teacher to Do?

• In a BAM!radio podcast I hosted on this topic, Launa recommended that, "If teachers' districts are mandating increasingly realistic active shooter drills, I encourage them to initiate courageous conversations. The supposed safety increases from such drills come at a significant cost; each drill ebbs away the safe learning environment that educators strive daily to create for their students."

(Continued)

(Continued)

• Launa also suggests that teachers and parents pressure elected representatives to advocate for sensible gun legislation.

• Amanda Nickerson, a professor of educational psychology who has studied the effects of safety drills on kids, was another guest on that episode. She stated, "Schools should begin with discussion and orientation with the staff so that they can model calm and confidence in carrying out the drills in developmentally appropriate ways. Students should be informed that these drills provide them with tools to be as safe as possible in the very unlikely event that there is danger. Educators should be aware of possible traumatic reactions, monitor the students for these, and provide access to appropriate mental health support if needed."

• Lesley Koplow, an educator and clinical social worker and the third guest on the above-mentioned episode, advised that teachers use books to support children after safety drills. Her suggestions for Pre-K and kindergarten include:

  • *I Will Keep You Safe and Sound*, by Lori Haskins Houran
  • *Safe, Warm and Snug*, by Stephen Swinburne
  • *Inch and Roly and the Very Small Hiding Place*, by Melissa Wiley
  • *Bear Feels Scared*, by Karma Wilson

For first and second grade, she recommends:

  • *The Best Nest*, by Doris L. Mueller
  • *Over and Under the Snow*, by Kate Messner
  • *Sometimes I'm Scared*, by Jane Annunziata and Marc Nemiroff

Where to Learn More

- The National Association of School Psychologists offers detailed guidance about conducting drills here:

  https://www.nasponline.org/resources-and-publications/
  resources-and-podcasts/school-climate-safety-and-crisis/
  systems-level-prevention/best-practice-considerations-
  for-schools-in-active-shooter-and-other-armed-assailant-
  drills

- You'll find an NPR piece titled "Experts Worry Active Shooter Drills in Schools Could Be Traumatic for Students" here:

  https://www.npr.org/2019/11/10/778015261/experts-worry-
  active-shooter-drills-in-schools-could-be-traumatic-for-
  students

- Launa Hall's piece can be found here:

  https://www.washingtonpost.com/opinions/rehearsing-
  for-death-a-pre-k-teacher-on-the-trouble-with-lockdown-
  drills/2014/10/28/4ab456ea-5eb2-11e4-9f3a-7e28799e0549_
  story.html

- You can read Sergio Pecanha's piece here:

  https://www.washingtonpost.com/opinions/2019/10/11/
  lockdown-drills-an-american-quirk-out-control/?arc404=
  true

  This article provides statistics offering some perspective on the need for lockdown drills.

- *Education Week* offers "'I Worry Every Day': Lockdown Drills Prompt Fear, Self-Reflection After School Shooting." You can read it here:

  https://www.edweek.org/ew/articles/2018/02/20/theyre-
  coming-for-me-and-my-kids.html

- Listen to the BAM!radio podcast titled "Rehearsing for Death: Shifting to Safety Drills That Do No Harm" here:

  https://www.bamradionetwork.com/track/rehearsing-for-
  death-shifting-to-safety-drills-that-do-no-harm/

CHAPTER 29

Advocating for Children Can Be an Uphill Battle

Do you know the story of Sisyphus? In Greek mythology, this former king of Corinth was punished in Hades by continually having to roll a huge boulder up a hill only to have it roll back down as soon as he got it to the summit. I'm sure many of us have felt that way at certain times in our lives, but perhaps no one feels it more than the person advocating for children—especially if that advocacy involves play.

As I wrote in *What If Everybody Understood Child Development?*, I'm not sure when play became a "four-letter word." And I'm really not sure why we in this country insist upon practices—that is, sitting and testing—that have been shown to be ineffectual. They say the definition of insanity is doing the same thing over and over again and expecting different results. Well, here we not only do it over and over again; also, we do *more* of it. It's insanity on steroids.

Last year, I received an email from a distraught mother who also happens to be a teacher. The school her child attends, and where she teaches, had reduced recess for Pre-K and kindergarten students to *10 minutes a day*. The reason, of course, was to "optimize instructional time"—one of my least favorite phrases in the English language.

Not surprisingly, by November of that school year, this woman—let's call her Mary—noticed severe behavioral issues in her young daughter, including irritability, lack of motivation to attend school, meltdowns, and exhaustion. And Mary heard from several teachers that other students—especially those with ADHD—were being similarly affected.

Mary did everything I would have advised if someone asked me how to become an advocate. She brought the issue to her principal and spoke at length about the negative impact of the limited outdoor time. When she was told he couldn't make changes to the schedule without permission from the central office, she began gathering research on best practices, play-based learning, and developmentally appropriate strategies for young children. She brought all of this to the assistant superintendent. And, although he expressed genuine interest and gave the impression that the situation could be easily addressed, recess time remained the same.

Her next meeting was with the superintendent. At this point, Mary not only had research with her; also, she'd gathered data from a "day of play," during which teachers filled out a form she'd created, documenting evidence of learning through play. The three-hour meeting proved futile, with her superintendent informing her "you can use research to prove anything." And when she asked to be placed on the agenda for the next school board meeting, Mary was denied.

Ultimately, she went to the school board meeting anyway, info in hand and supporters in attendance, and was allowed two minutes to make her case. Sadly, nothing changed for the children.

Mary confided to me that, on more than one occasion, she was asked to drop the issue. And immediately following the school board meeting, her superintendent tried to get her transferred. Mary felt she had committed career suicide, but she assured me that despite her low morale and the now-toxic environment at school, her belief in the cause—the children's mental health—would keep her going. At a later date, I reached out to learn the results of her second school board appearance but never did hear back from her.

At this point you may be wondering why, exactly, I'm sharing this story. As of yet, it doesn't have a happy ending.

In fact, it may lean more toward the tragic. But I do want to communicate the fact that there *are* passionate people out there who care very deeply for children and are fighting for what's right for them.

I also want to convey that, in advocating for children, it's important to use whatever tools are available to us. That should include putting ourselves in the shoes of those with whom we're debating, no matter how wrong their thinking may be. With that in mind, I advised Mary to use not just research on the value of play but also on the contributions of recess to improved academic performance.

Yes, it ticks me off that we have to do that. But the truth is, recess does contribute greatly to academic performance and there's plenty of research proving it. And while Mary's superintendent might dismiss research concerning the benefits of play in general—something for which she obviously holds no value—she would probably be less inclined to snub information concerning better test scores and grades, as these are commodities that clearly matter to her.

Whatever methods we use, we simply have to keep battling for what's best for children. We have to believe that, unlike Sisyphus, we *will* get the boulder to the summit!

What's a Teacher to Do?

- As frustrating and unfortunate as it may be, we have to consider "WIFM" ("what's in it for me?"), as most people are more inclined to respond to how something benefits *them*. Sadly, that means arguing in favor of something that benefits the children may not get the hoped-for results. In the case of Mary's superintendent, better test scores and grades were clearly of greater importance than the benefits of play to children. So, when preparing your case, consider what may be in it for the person or people to whom you're presenting it.

(Continued)

(Continued)

- Focus on one issue at a time.

- Tell stories! It's necessary to present data, but if you can accompany that data with a story, you'll be much more effective. Even if administrators and policymakers have a me-first (or a testing-first) attitude, they're probably not heartless. In Mary's case, I hope she told the story of her daughter's decline. But including similar stories of other children—so she wouldn't seem to be advocating for her child only—might have had more impact.

- Don't go it alone. Mary made herself a target for her administration, putting her job in jeopardy. But had she enlisted the help of other like-minded teachers, as well as parents, she would have been more empowered. A principal or superintendent may be willing to rid himself of one "bad apple," but in reality couldn't consider firing several teachers.

- If at all possible, invite decision-makers to witness what's happening. Ask them to join you and the children for a 10-minute recess, for example, so they can experience just how limited it is. How little it offers the children. They say that seeing is believing. We have to hope that's true.

- At the request of early childhood professionals, I created reproducible brochures that can inform decision-makers on commonly misunderstood topics. They include Why Play Matters, Why Recess Matters, Sitting Does Not Equal Learning, Worksheets Do Not Equal Learning, Earlier Isn't Better, and What You Should Know About Screen Use. These trifold brochures are in PDF form and can be reproduced as often as necessary, for as long as necessary. The messages are brief, include pertinent research, and can be helpful when teachers feel the messaging is more likely to be heard if it comes from an outside source. If you think they might be helpful, you can learn more about them here:

  https://www.raepica.com/reproducible-brochures-for-administrators-policymakers/

Where to Learn More

- Read "The Role of Advocacy in Public Education," written by a teacher:

  https://www.advanc-ed.org/source/role-advocacy-public-education

- NAEYC offers many resources regarding advocacy. You can learn more here:

  https://www.naeyc.org/our-work/public-policy-advocacy/build-your-advocacy-skills-and-knowledge

- The McCormick Center for Early Childhood Leadership is another great resource. Check out their "Early Childhood Advocacy for Beginners" here:

  https://mccormickcenter.nl.edu/library/early-childhood-advocacy-for-beginners-part-i/

CHAPTER 30

What If Early Childhood Professionals Pushed Back?

In the last chapter I wrote about the uphill battle of advocating for children—especially around the topic of play. But, as you know, our battles these days concern not just play but also developmentally appropriate practice in general. Sad but true.

This hit home when I was conducting my third professional development training for a Virginia school district. In the middle of one of my points, one young woman raised her hand and asked, "Why are you here?" Not exactly the kind of question I was expecting.

My confusion was obvious (I'm rarely speechless), so she expounded. "You come here and share all of these ideas of things we should be doing with the kids," she said, "but what good is it if the county isn't going to let us do them?"

Wow.

That was a first. But I had to admit she had a point. What good is it, indeed, if the end result is only going to be frustration? Earlier in the day, in fact, another teacher had commented that she'd been "dinged" by her principal for doing one of the activities I shared the last time I was there.

Rarely, if ever, do I get to hear such things—because it's rare for me to work with teachers more than once. They generally don't become comfortable enough to make such comments aloud. Plenty of teachers may have had these thoughts throughout the years, but that's usually as far as it goes.

I have to say, as hard as it is to hear comments like these, I'm very grateful to the two teachers who spoke up. I need to consider such issues. But I'm *really* grateful to another young (and feisty) teacher who also addressed the group—because she gave me even more food for thought. She said, "So what if they ding you? What are they going to do, fire you? They can't hire enough teachers these days!"

We all had a good laugh. But considering it later, I realized that these opposite viewpoints represent two categories of early childhood professionals currently occupying classrooms. The first is the teacher who *knows* developmentally appropriate practice and is frustrated—often beyond tears—by her inability to offer it to the children. The second is the teacher who, when asked to implement developmentally *in*appropriate practices, does what she knows to be best anyway, damn the consequences.

Now, I realize it's easy for me to say that we need far more of the second type. I'm self-employed and accountable only to myself. But I once heard a colleague say, "Teachers have been told for too long to shut up and do their job—and for too long they've done just that." And I have to wonder: What if they hadn't? What if they'd adopted the attitude of that feisty teacher in my training? What if they'd put the children's needs first and foremost and stood up to those administrators who tried to bully them into harmful teaching practices?

Although they may not have sworn the Hippocratic oath, as doctors do, I believe teachers in the trenches must also abide by the pledge to "first do no harm."

Again, I realize it's easier for me to push back than it is for someone whose livelihood may be threatened. So, for those in fear of losing their jobs, I have two suggestions.

The first is that you not stand alone. When teachers in Seattle decided to push back against the Measure of Academic Progress (MAP) test, they risked suspension or other disciplinary actions. But they banded together, garnering the support of parents and students and, eventually, thanks to social media, educators throughout the state and country. And they won their battle! It's a wonderful story of the power of teachers who believed in what they were fighting for. A few years later, striking Seattle teachers refused to settle until all elementary students were guaranteed 30 minutes of daily recess. Again, they won the battle.

My second suggestion, for those unwilling to engage in all-out war, is that you arm yourself with as much information as possible. Yes, I'm talking about research; we should always be armed with that. But I also mean that when an administrator comes to you and asks, "Why are you doing *this stuff?*" you will have an answer that is specific to the activity you're doing.

For example, if the children are making geometric shapes with their bodies, you can tell your administrator exactly which math standard is being addressed. If the children are playing a cooperative game, you can point out the social studies standard it complements. If they are stomping, slithering, and stalking, you can specify exactly which literacy standard, relevant to word comprehension, is behind the activity.

I can't guarantee you'll get the results you're/we're hoping for. But at least you'll know you tried. That you didn't just "shut up and do your job." And if you *keep* trying—and provide evidence that it *works*—you never know what miracles may occur.

Yes, it's scary to push back. But the children are worth it. And at the end of the day, you'll know you did your best to do no harm.

What's a Teacher to Do?

• Seek out other like-minded teachers in your school or district so you know you're not alone.

• Find support among your personal learning network (PLN) on social media.

• Collect as much research as possible—both general and specific to your activities—so you have an answer to a question such as, "Why are you doing this stuff?"

(Continued)

(Continued)

- Educate parents! Many have no idea of the developmentally inappropriate practices going on in their children's schools. Most will be appalled if they comprehend how wrong it is, and they will stand with you if or when you need their support. To help parents better understand developmentally appropriate practice, you can use these reproducible parent letters that explain, in one page, such issues as why earlier isn't better, why you don't use worksheets, and more: https://www.raepica.com/reproducible-parent-letters/

- "Sneak" active learning experiences into the classroom whenever possible (see Chapter 18).

- Use NAEYC's book, *Developmentally Appropriate Practice in Early Childhood Programs*, to defend your position.

- If you find your words go in one ear and out the other when talking to your administrators, provide words from an outside source via these reproducible brochures: https://www.raepica.com/reproducible-brochures-for-administrators-policymakers/.

Where to Learn More

- The 12-minute podcast, "ECE Advocacy 101: You're Either at the Table or on the Menu," offers lots of wonderful advice from the directors of four state AEYC organizations:

  http://www.bamradionetwork.com/naeyc-radio/1008-ece-advocacy-101-youre-either-at-the-table-or-on-the-menu

- Watch the six-minute video called "5 Ways to Sneak Movement Into the Curriculum":

  https://www.youtube.com/watch?v=I1StHBuzoPs

- Peter Gray's article, "K & Preschool Teachers: Last Stand in War on Childhood?," provides emotional support:

  https://www.psychologytoday.com/us/blog/freedom-learn/201507/k-preschool-teachers-last-stand-in-war-childhood?fbclid=IwAR0NbA-kYhDh7XLvMyjAgTJlHWFfvy2y4t24HPMwh4vTHlTQNq6DrFPBDc8

CHAPTER 31

ECE Advocacy: We Have the Numbers and the Tools

Because I speak at so many conferences, I rarely choose to attend one where I'm not presenting. But one Saturday, Northern Virginia Association for the Education of Young Children (NVAEYC) hosted a half-day summit on advocacy—a topic that has become increasingly important to me—so I decided I had to be there. And I'm glad I went.

As I wrote previously, it can be challenging to advocate. It can feel as though you're beating your head against a wall—or, as I said, as though you're Sisyphus endlessly pushing that boulder up a steep hill. Whether we're talking about advocating for early childhood education to be taken seriously, for better pay for its professionals, or for the return of developmental appropriateness (and sanity) to policy and practices, it often seems as though no one is paying attention. That's why I was so happy to see that among the speakers at the summit was a panel of state senators and delegates. They'd given up part of their weekend to listen! How refreshing.

The morning was informative. I made a lot of notes as these government representatives were addressing us. But the comment beside which I placed a star was this one: "Policymakers need to understand how important an issue is so they'll direct their attention to it."

That makes a lot of sense. Policymakers have a great deal on their plates and many people clamoring for their attention. It means, of course, that unless we're among those who speak up, we risk being forever overlooked.

I realize just the idea of speaking up can be intimidating for many, perhaps especially among early childhood educators. You went into this field because you love young children; you're not necessarily comfortable as a "warrior." But, truly, advocacy can be a lot less intimidating than you might imagine.

For one thing, you can take comfort in the fact that you are not alone. I often tell early childhood professionals that there are more of us than them! With numbers comes power. It's important to keep that in mind when we feel intimidated.

Among our numbers are groups such as Defending the Early Years, a nonprofit organization working for a just, equitable, and quality early childhood education for every child. They publish reports, make mini-documentaries, issue position statements, advocate on policy, and have a website full of resources, blogs, and activist steps for early childhood professionals.

And at that advocacy summit, I learned about a fairly new initiative from the National Association for the Education of Young Children (NAEYC). It's America for Early Ed, a national campaign to ensure that candidates and policymakers from both sides of the aisle recognize and embrace early learning as a "must." This group is mobilizing the early childhood profession and its allies to advocate at the local, state, and federal levels for an increased and sustainable investment in early childhood education.

Margaret Mead said, "Never doubt that a small group of thoughtful, committed citizens can change the world; indeed, it's the only thing that ever has." Just imagine what a large group of us can do!

What's a Teacher to Do?

• Be able to clearly articulate why your topic of choice matters. NVAEYC proposed creating and practicing an elevator speech—a short statement you can make in the time it takes an elevator to move between floors.

• Become a story collector. Your stories, and those of others, put "a face" on early childhood education and can back up the data, which Lucy Recio, NAEYC's Senior Analyst for Public Policy and Advocacy, maintains is "the backbone of any advocacy strategy."

• Talk to people—especially those outside of the field—about the positive work early childhood educators are doing. Among those you can tell your stories to are members of church communities, parents, and professionals who are part of your local upper elementary and high school community, and those involved in higher education. Next time you're riding with Uber or Lyft, strike up a conversation with the driver! And don't forget business leaders. Lucy emphasized that they can be among our most effective allies because they're aware of the dollars lost when parents are without childcare.

• If we want the early childhood profession to be taken seriously and respected, never doubt for a moment that language matters. You are a *teacher* or an *educator*, not a "daycare worker," for example, and certainly not a babysitter! Also, if you're in a center, as opposed to a public or private school, don't refer to it as a "daycare" center. Nobody is taking care of days. You should call it a childcare or early learning center.

• Maximize social media, even for connecting with government officials.

• Use Resistbot to get in touch with elected officials.

(Continued)

(Continued)

- If you're going to contact someone about a particular issue, be sure you know who to contact about what. Some people are responsible for appropriations, others for policy. At what level are the decisions being made? You want to be sure you're not wasting anybody's time, yours included.

- Vote, vote, vote! And before you do, make sure you know a candidate's position regarding early education.

Where to Learn More

- Defending the Early Years offers an advocacy kit, as well as additional resources, here:

  https://dey.org/activists-tool-kit/

- Here's another early childhood advocacy toolkit:

  https://www.theounce.org/wp-content/uploads/2017/03/EarlyChildhoodAdvocacyToolkit.pdf

- You can learn about America for Early Ed here:

  http://www.americaforearlyed.org/

- You can learn about Resistbot here:

  https://resist.bot/

References
and Resources

Chapter 1

Article

- You can access a paper titled "From Positive Reinforcement to Positive Behaviors: An Everyday Guide for the Practitioner," written by Ellen Ava Sigler and Shirley Aamidor, here: https://link.springer.com/article/10.1007%2Fs10643-004-0753-9. The paper appeared in *Early Childhood Education Journal.*

Podcast

- Listen to the podcast "Creating Praise Junkies: Are You Giving Too Much 'Positive Reinforcement'?" Ellen Ava Sigler is a guest. It can be accessed here: https://www.bamradionetwork.com/track/creating-praise-junkies-are-you-giving-children-too-much-positive-reinforcement/

Videos

- Part 1 of Diane Sawyer's special can be found here: https://www.youtube.com/watch?v=GqeOWatgN9w&list=PLQOa26lW-uI-pNs2w7ie09BET5LY_xDOF
- In this minute-and-a-half video, a dad carries on a conversation with his baby boy, who can't even speak yet: https://www.youtube.com/watch?v=AY35eXTKVLY. The video made the rounds on Facebook and was enormously popular among early childhood professionals. I suspect the reason it went viral is because it's so cute. But I was also struck by the good fortune of the baby involved. Not only is

he learning a great deal about quality communication; also, getting so much of his dad's attention has to make him feel pretty darn special.

Chapter 2

Articles

- The American Academy of Pediatrics offers "The Importance of Play in Healthy Child Development and Maintaining Strong Parent-Child Bonds": https://pediatrics.aappublications.org/content/119/1/182
- Here's information about the study, conducted by University of Virginia researchers, demonstrating that kindergarten has become the new first grade: http://www.aera.net/Newsroom/News-Releases-and-Statements/Study-Snapshot-Is-Kindergarten-the-New-First-Grade
- Read "Why Your Brain Needs More Downtime": https://www.scientificamerican.com/article/mental-downtime/
- Read "'Schools Are Killing Curiosity': Why We Need to Stop Telling Children to Shut Up and Learn": https://www.theguardian.com/education/2020/jan/28/schools-killing-curiosity-learn
- Read "The Scary, Lasting Effects of Too Much Screen Time on Children": https://www.marketwatch.com/story/the-scary-lasting-effects-of-too-much-screen-time-on-children-2019-04-10
- "Two Hours Screen Time Linked to Children's Behavior Problems" can be accessed here: https://www.techtimes.com/articles/241842/20190419/two-hours-screen-time-linked-to-childrens-behavioral-problems.htm

Books

- *Acting Out!: Avoid Behavior Challenges With Active Learning Games & Activities* offers research and advice on the topic of challenging behavior, along with 200 activities that promote community building, prosocial skills, self-regulation, and relaxation.

- Alfie Kohn's *No Contest: The Case Against Competition* is probably the quintessential book on the topic of competition.
- To learn more about the role of the body in learning, you might read Eric Jensen's *Learning With the Body in Mind* or John Ratey's *Spark: The Revolutionary New Science of Exercise and the Brain.*

Podcast

- Nancy Carlsson-Paige discusses children's current inability to play in this 11-minute podcast: https://www.bamradio network.com/track/have-children-lost-their-ability-to-play/

Chapter 3
Article

- For information on how a lack of movement is impacting the development of the proprioceptive and vestibular systems, read "The Shocking Phenomenon That Shows Just How Movement-Starved Modern Kids Really Are": https://www.stack.com/a/the-shocking-phenomenon-that-shows-just-how-movement-starved-modern-kids-really-are

Books

- Angela Hansom's book *Balanced and Barefoot* does an excellent job helping us understand why children can't sit still, pay attention, and so forth. Angela is a pediatric occupational therapist and knows what she's talking about.
- For straight talk about bettering children's lives and education—and better understanding young children— read *What If Everybody Understood Child Development?*, published by Corwin.

Course

- I've created a two-hour online course titled "Avoid Challenging Behavior in Your Early Childhood Setting." You can find it here: https://raepica.teachable.com/p/avoid-challenging-behavior-in-early-childhood-settings

Chapter 4

Articles

- This article provides an overview of a study showing a correlation between stronger connections with parents and reduced preschool expulsions: https://www.educationdive .com/news/study-to-reduce-preschool-expulsions-form-stronger-connections-with-paren/551763/
- An article in *The Wall Street Journal*, although an opinion piece, offers information regarding studies on the topic. Titled "We're Overmedicating Our Children," it can be found here: https://www.wsj.com/articles/were-overmedicating-our-children-11551917025

Podcast

- It behooves all of us to reflect on our potential biases. In this 11-minute podcast, Rosemarie Allen and educator Jason Flom discuss the question, "Do You Treat Black and White Students Differently?": https://www.bamradionetwork.com/ track/do-you-treat-black-and-white-students-differently/

Videos

- Walter Gilliam is the ultimate expert on the subject of preschool expulsions. This nine-minute video featuring Dr. Gilliam provides a brief overview of who's being expelled and why: https://www.youtube.com/watch?v=EQqAQgBwJxY
- Watch Rosemarie Allen's TEDx Talk, "School Suspensions Are an Adult Behavior": https://www.youtube.com/ watch?v=f8nkcRMZKV4. Dr. Allen tells her audience that from the time she entered school, she was suspended at least seven times a year!

Chapter 5

Articles

- *Young Children*, the journal of NAEYC, offers an article called "Reducing Challenging Behaviors During Transitions: Strategies for Early Childhood Educators to Share

With Parents." You'll find it here: https://www.naeyc.org/
resources/pubs/yc/sep2018/reducing-challenging-behaviors-
during-transitions

Book

- You'll find even more transition activities in my book,
  *Teachable Transitions: 190 Activities to Move From
  Morning Circle to the End of the Day.*

Course

- "Make Transitions Trouble-Free & Teachable!" is an
  online course for early childhood professionals. It reviews
  the trouble with traditional transitions, explores how transitions can be linked to learning, and offers tips for making
  transitions chaos-free and fun, as well as numerous suggested transition activities: https://raepica.teachable.com/p/
  make-transitions-trouble-free-teachable/

Podcast

- Listen to the 11-minute podcast, "Creating Trouble-Free
  Transitions," involving four early childhood professionals:
  https://www.bamradionetwork.com/track/creating-trouble-
  free-transitions-2/

Video

- There are many ideas for transition activities, for different
  parts of the day, on my YouTube channel: https://www.you
  tube.com/channel/UC-d20r_dzRuJdQ7J0TEZOMQ

Chapter 6

Article

- Information about Skibbe's research can be found in "The
  Child's Ability to Self-Regulate Is a Critical Element in
  Childhood Language and Literacy Development": https://
  theeconomyofmeaning.com/2018/06/04/the-childs-ability-to-
  self-regulate-is-a-critical-element-in-childhood-language-and-
  literacy-development/

Book

- *Acting Out!: Avoid Behavior Challenges With Active Learning Games & Activities* by Rae Pica includes a chapter of games that foster self-regulation.

Podcast

- Although intended primarily for parents (and misnamed), there's much good information in this podcast interview called "Teaching Children Self-Control," with psychology professor Laura Berk: https://www.bamradionetwork.com/track/teaching-children-self-control-2/

Videos

- Videos with game suggestions are available on the YouTube channel *Active Learning With Rae*: https://www.youtube.com/channel/UC-d20r_dzRuJdQ7J0TEZOMQ

Chapter 7

Articles

- Responsive Classroom has an excellent article, "Punishment vs. Logical Consequences," at https://www.responsiveclassroom.org/punishment-vs-logical-consequences/
- Education World offers a series of three helpful articles on logical consequences. The first is "Logical Consequences Teach Important Lessons": https://www.educationworld.com/a_curr/columnists/charney/charney005.shtml. The second is "The Three R's of Logical Consequences": https://www.educationworld.com/a_curr/columnists/charney/charney006.shtml. The final piece is "Examples of Logical Consequences": https://www.educationworld.com/a_curr/columnists/charney/charney007.shtml.

Book

- An excellent source for understanding the role of culture in teaching is Zaretta Hammond's *Culturally Responsive Teaching and the Brain*.

Podcast

- You can listen to Dr. Muriel Rand, author of *The Positive Classroom* and *The Positive Preschool*, and educator/director Jason Flom discuss "Logical Consequences: Nuanced Responses to Student Misbehavior" here: https://www.bamradionetwork.com/track/logical-consequences-nuanced-responses-to-student-behavior/

Chapter 8

Articles

- You can find information about blue light and vision here: https://www.reviewofoptometry.com/article/seeing-blue-the-impact-of-excessive-blue-light-exposure
- Here's information regarding a 2016 study demonstrating the increase in childhood myopia: https://news.usc.edu/91007/usc-eye-institute-study-seeks-cures-to-childhood-myopia/
- Read "Too Much Screen Time Linked to an Epidemic of Myopia Among Young People" here: https://medicalxpress.com/news/2019-02-screen-linked-epidemic-myopia-young.html
- Here's a CNN report about Dr. Catherine Birken's 2017 study concerning screen use and communication delays: https://www.cnn.com/2017/05/04/health/babies-screen-time-speech-delays-study/index.html
- "MRIs Show Screen Time Linked to Lower Brain Development in Preschoolers" can be found here: https://www.cnn.com/2019/11/04/health/screen-time-lower-brain-development-preschoolers-wellness/index.html

Podcast

- Cindy joins Dr. Victoria Dunckley, author of *Reset Your Child's Brain*, and education leader Jill Berkowicz for a discussion about the impact of screen time on students here: https://www.bamradionetwork.com/track/do-you-know-enough-about-the-impact-of-screen-time-on-students/

Website

- Cindy Eckard's website has an abundance of valuable advice. You'll find it here: http://www.screensandkids.us/

Chapter 9

Articles

- Dr. Peter Gray writes about "The Decline of Play and Rise in Children's Mental Disorders" here: https://www.psychologytoday.com/us/blog/freedom-learn/201001/the-decline-play-and-rise-in-childrens-mental-disorders
- Read "The Virtues of Daydreaming" here: https://www.newyorker.com/tech/frontal-cortex/the-virtues-of-daydreaming and "The Upside of Downtime" here: https://hbr.org/2012/12/the-upside-of-downtime
- This piece in *Scientific American* explains "Why Your Brain Needs Downtime": https://www.scientificamerican.com/article/mental-downtime/
- For an excellent overview on children's need for downtime, read "Is Your Child Getting Enough Real Downtime?": https://health.usnews.com/wellness/for-parents/articles/2017-09-28/is-your-child-getting-enough-real-downtime. It's written by child psychologist Dr. Susan Bartell.
- "Teach Kids to Daydream" is an excellent resource. You'll find it here: https://www.theatlantic.com/education/archive/2013/10/teach-kids-to-daydream/280615/

Podcasts

- You can listen to my conversation about the impact of sleep deprivation on the classroom, with Dr. Mary Sheedy Kurcinka, Dr. James Maas, and two educators, here: https://www.bamradionetwork.com/track/five-classroom-problems-directly-traceable-to-student-sleep-deprivation/
- I talk with Dr. Mary Helen Immordino-Yang about the value of daydreaming in class in this 12-minute podcast: https://www.bamradionetwork.com/track/students-daydreaming-in-class-it-s-productive-if/

Chapter 10

Articles

- The article to which I refer at the beginning of the chapter can be found here: https://www.stack.com/a/the-shocking-phenomenon-that-shows-just-how-movement-starved-modern-kids-really-are?fbclid=IwAR2h6ap3etBUhEA-1oKlhrlY318WkCBQBMdJkkubJqn_oogPqEtvfxaKe2A
- There's information about the proprioceptive and vestibular senses, including ways to promote it, in this article called "The Sixth and Seventh Senses": https://eyaslanding.com/the-vestibular-and-proprioceptive-systems-the-sixth-and-seven-senses/

Book

- Read Angela Hanscom's excellent book, *Balanced and Barefoot: How Unrestricted Outdoor Play Makes for Strong, Confident and Capable Children.*

Video

- Watch Angela's TEDx Talk, only seven and a half minutes long, for better understanding of how the lack of movement in children's lives is impacting the ability to learn: https://www.ted.com/talks/angela_hanscom_the_real_reason_children_fidget_and_what_we_can_do_about_it

Chapter 11

Articles

- You can read "Preschool Kids Starved for Exercise" here: https://www.usatoday.com/story/news/2015/05/18/preschoolers-not-exercising/27396311/
- The *U.S. News & World Report* can be found here: https://health.usnews.com/health-news/articles/2015/05/18/preschoolers-arent-getting-enough-physical-activity-in-child-care

Books

- John Ratey's book, *Spark: The Revolutionary New Science of Exercise and the Brain*, although published in 2008, still offers the ultimate explanation of the science behind the mind/body connection.

- My book, *Great Games for Young Children*, offers more than 100 games that can be played both inside and outside.

Miscellaneous

- Read the research brief, "Active Education: Growing Evidence on Physical Activity and Academic Performance," here: https://activelivingresearch.org/sites/active livingresearch.org/files/ALR_Brief_ActiveEducation_Jan 2015.pdf
- You can find information regarding SHAPE America's physical activity guidelines here: https://www.shape america.org/standards/guidelines/. Included on the site is information about *Active Start: A Statement of Physical Activity Guidelines for Children From Birth to Age 5* (https://www.shapeamerica.org/standards/guidelines/ activestart.aspx) and a statement of guidelines for children 5–12 (https://www.shapeamerica.org/standards/guidelines/ pa-children-5-12.aspx).

Chapter 12

Books

- My book, *Acting Out!: Avoid Behavior Challenges With Active Learning Games & Activities*, offers additional tips, along with circle games, cooperative activities, brain breaks, and more.
- You can't go wrong with Eric Jensen's *Learning With the Body in Mind: The Scientific Basis for Energizers, Movement, Play, and Physical Education*.
- *Think of Something Quiet*, written by the late Clare Cherry, has been around since 1981 but perhaps now is more relevant and needed than ever. It offers early childhood educators strategies for achieving a low-stress classroom environment.

Course

- My online course called "Avoid Challenging Behavior in Your Early Childhood Setting" can be found here: https:// raepica.teachable.com/p/avoid-challenging-behavior-in-early-childhood-settings

Podcast

- Listen to this conversation on the Not Just Cute podcast about how movement helps us avoid behavior challenges: https://notjustcute.com/podcast/episode29/

Chapter 13

Articles

- Here's the link to the British study to which I referred: https://www.dailymail.co.uk/health/article-2229567/The-children-held-school-lazy-lifestyles-mean-t-stand-leg.html
- "Make Active Play Part of Your Day" outlines some of the health hazards of sedentary behaviors: https://www.raepica.com/2017/08/make-active-play-part-day/
- Learn about a study titled "Associations Between Sedentary Behavior and Motor Coordination in Children" here: https://onlinelibrary.wiley.com/doi/abs/10.1002/ajhb.22310

Podcasts

- Listen to an 11-minute podcast called "Solving the Growing Physical Activity Crisis": https://www.bamradio network.com/track/solving-the-growing-physical-activity-crisis/
- Another relevant podcast is "Fitting Fitness Into the Curriculum": https://www.bamradionetwork.com/track/fitting-fitness-into-the-curriculum/

Chapter 14

Articles

- For more on the mind-body connection, read "Do the Children in Your Classrooms Have Bodies?": https://www.raepica.com/2017/12/mind-body-connection/
- "Effect of Ability to Cross Midline on Performance of Handwriting" can be downloaded here: https://scholar works.wmich.edu/ot_posters/39/

Book

- Carla Hannaford's *Smart Moves: Why Learning Is Not All in Your Head* is my favorite professional book. I wish every educator and parent could read it.

Miscellaneous

- To learn about Brain Gym: www.braingym.org
- This Pinterest page offers ideas and resources: https://www.pinterest.com/growhandsonkids/crossing-midline-activities/

Video

- For activity ideas involving crossing the midline, check out my YouTube video, "Emergent Literacy: Why Cross-Lateral Movement Matters!": https://www.youtube.com/watch?v=yrYMIcXC9Yw&t=11s

Chapter 15

Article

- For information on the screen-time study, read "Screen Time for Kids Under 2 More Than Doubles, Study Finds": https://www.cnn.com/2019/02/18/health/kids-screen-time-tv-study/index.html

Books

- Christy Isbell's book *Mighty Fine Motor Fun: Fine Motor Activities for Young Children* offers the support and tools teachers need to teach fine motor skills.
- A second resource is *Basics of Fine Motor Skills: Developmental Activities for Kids*, written by Heather Greutman and intended for parents, educators, and therapists.

Podcasts

- Listen to "Fine Motor Skills: What Are They? Why Are They Too Important to Overlook?", a 10-minute podcast featuring Christy Isbell, kindergarten teacher Allison

Sampish, and early childhood expert Deborah Stewart: http://www.bamradionetwork.com/educators-channel/774-fine-motor-skills-what-are-they-why-are-they-too-important-to-overlook
- A second relevant podcast is "Introducing Writing Skills to Young Children," with pediatric occupational therapist Angela Hanscom and early childhood expert Amanda Morgan: http://www.bamradionetwork.com/student-centric-strategies/4287-introducing-writing-skills-to-very-young-children

Chapter 16

Articles

- You can read Angela Hansom's "The Real Reason Why Kids Fidget" here: https://www.huffpost.com/entry/the-real-reason-why-kids-fidget_b_5586265
- Read "Kids Who Can't Sit Still," which references the 2008 study, here: http://www.nea.org/tools/47003.htm
- The 2015 study headed by Dr. Dustin Sarver is explained here: https://www.umc.edu/news/News_Articles/2015/April/Researcher–Hyperactive-movements-help-ADHD-children-learn.html

Podcast

- Dr. Dustin Sarver and Angela Hanscom are guests on this podcast episode titled "Why Students Fidget in Class: Abnormal and Distracting or Normal and Desirable?": https://www.bamradionetwork.com/track/why-students-fidget-in-class-abnormal-and-distracting-or-normal-and-desirable-2/

Chapter 17

Articles

- More thoughts and recommendations are available on this blog post written by an educator: https://applesand bananaseducation.com/criss-cross-applesauce-obsolete/
- Here are even more thoughts on the topic from early childhood educator Deborah Stewart: https://teachpre school.org/2019/07/02/i-cannot-sit-crisscross-applesauce-with-my-hands-in-my-lap/

Podcast

- Listen to the above-mentioned podcast, "Teaching Strategies: Handling Young Students Who Just Won't Sit Still": https://www.bamradionetwork.com/track/teaching-strategies handling-young-students-who-just-wont-sit-still-2/

Chapter 18

Books

- *Acting Out!: Avoid Behavior Challenges With Active Games & Activities* offers circle games for building community and includes a chapter on brain breaks. Eric Jensen's *Learning With the Body in Mind* also includes brain breaks (what he calls energizers), as well as rationale for them.
- My book *Active Learning Across the Curriculum* offers hundreds of activities under the content areas of art, emergent literacy, math, music, science, and social studies. Another possibility is *The Kinesthetic Classroom* by Traci Lengel and Mike Kuczala.
- My book *Teachable Transitions* offers 190 activities to help children transition creatively from arrival to departure.

Course

- "Make Transitions Trouble-Free & Teachable" is an online course for early childhood professionals. It offers many activities for the six typical daily transitions and can be found here: https://raepica.teachable.com/p/make-transitions-trouble-free-teachable/

Podcast

- Listen to "Fitting Fitness Into the Curriculum" here: https://www.bamradionetwork.com/track/fitting-fitness-into-the-curriculum/

Video

- My YouTube channel offers many videos on brain breaks, active learning, transitions, and more. You can find it here: https://www.youtube.com/channel/UC-d20r_dzRuJdQ7J0T EZOMQ

Chapter 19

Books

- Written resources include MaryAnn Kohl's books, *Preschool Art: It's the Process, Not the Product* and *Primary Art: It's the Process, Not the Product*

Podcasts

- Listen to "Valuing and Enjoying the Process of Learning," a 17-minute podcast featuring early childhood expert Amanda Morgan: http://www.bamradionetwork.com/student-centric-strategies/4487-valuing-and-enjoying-the-process-of-learning
- Listen to "Is It Possible That Creativity Is Misunderstood and Undervalued?" This is a 10-minute conversation with educator Stacey Goodman and James C. Kaufman, a professor of educational psychology: http://www.bamradio network.com/educators-channel/2300-is-it-possible-that-creativity-is-misunderstood-and-undervalued

Chapter 20

Articles

- Educator John Spencer offers "7 Ways to Inspire Divergent Thinking in the Classroom": http://www.spencer author.com/divergent-thinking/
- The University of Texas at Austin offers a PDF titled "How to Teach: Divergent Thinking": https://faculty innovate.utexas.edu/sites/default/files/TeachingGuide_How toTeachDivergentThinking.pdf
- Dr. Alice Sterling Honig has written "How to Promote Creative Thinking" with young children in mind: https://www.researchgate.net/publication/281408290_How_to_promote_creative_thinking

Podcast

- This 13-minute podcast episode offers a lively panel discussion on "Teaching Creativity in a Climate That Discourages It": https://www.bamradionetwork.com/track/teaching-creativity-in-a-climate-that-discourages-it-2-2/

Video

- Watch Sir Ken Robinson's excellent TED Talk, "Do Schools Kill Creativity?" here: https://www.youtube.com/watch?v=iG9CE55wbtY

Chapter 21
Articles

- Although written specifically for parents, I highly recommend you read this *Slate* article: https://slate.com/human-interest/2017/11/how-to-stop-sexism-and-raise-a-son-who-respects-women.html
- Review the study "Teaching Children to Confront Peers' Sexist Remarks: Implications for Theories of Gender Development and Educational Practice" here: https://link.springer.com/article/10.1007/s11199-009-9634-4
- In a 2010 study, researchers asked preschool teachers to emphasize gender in one classroom for two weeks, testing the children's attitudes about gender before and after. You can find the abstract here: https://www.ncbi.nlm.nih.gov/pubmed/21077864

Podcast

- To listen to the 10-minute discussion that inspired this chapter, click here: https://www.bamradionetwork.com/track/gender-stereotypes-is-this-really-a-problem/

Chapter 22
Articles

- Read Dr. Peter Gray's "Risky Play: Why Children Love It and Need It": https://www.psychologytoday.com/us/blog/freedom-learn/201404/risky-play-why-children-love-it-and-need-it
- Dr. Mariana Brussoni offers "Why Kids Need Risk, Fear and Excitement in Play": http://theconversation.com/why-kids-need-risk-fear-and-excitement-in-play-81450

- Read "The Overprotected Kid" here: https://www.the atlantic.com/magazine/archive/2014/04/hey-parents-leave-those-kids-alone/358631/
- The *Journal of Applied Developmental Psychology* published a study called "Parental Influences on Toddlers' Injury-Risk Behaviors: Are Sons and Daughters Socialized Differently?" You can find the abstract here: https://www.sciencedirect.com/science/article/pii/S0193397399000155
- Caroline Paul's "Why Do We Teach Girls That It's Cute to Be Scared?" is a good read and includes studies that have demonstrated girls are cautioned more often than boys. You can read it here: https://www.nytimes.com/2016/02/21/opinion/sunday/why-do-we-teach-girls-that-its-cute-to-be-scared.html
- Information about a study titled "What Is the Relationship Between Risky Outdoor Play and Health in Children? A Systematic Review" can be found here: https://www.mdpi.com/1660-4601/12/6/6423

Book

- I highly recommend *The Coddling of the American Mind: How Good Intentions and Bad Ideas Are Setting Up a Generation for Failure*, by Greg Lukianoff and Jonathan Haidt.

Podcast

- Listen to "Risky Child's Play: The Good, the Bad, and the Mostly Good" on BAM!radio: https://www.bamradio network.com/track/risky-child-play-the-good-the-bad-and-the-ugly/

Chapter 23

Articles

- "Number of Children & Adolescents Taking Psychiatric Drugs in the U.S.": https://www.cchrint.org/psychiatric-drugs/children-on-psychiatric-drugs/

- Read "Not Just a Phase: Depression in Preschoolers" here: https://www.psychologytoday.com/us/blog/talking-about-trauma/201306/not-just-phase-depression-in-preschoolers
- Harvard's Center on the Developing Child offers an overview of early childhood mental health here: https://developingchild.harvard.edu/science/deep-dives/mental-health/
- Learn about the study "Associations Between Screen Time and Lower Psychological Well-Being Among Children and Adolescents: Evidence From a Population-Based Study" here: https://www.sciencedirect.com/science/article/pii/S2211335518301827
- For information on the above-mentioned study, as well as other information regarding the subject, read *Time*'s piece, "There's Worrying New Research About Kids' Screen Time and Their Mental Health": https://time.com/5437607/smartphones-teens-mental-health/

Chapter 24

Articles

- The National Education Association addresses "Recess Before Lunch" here: http://www.nea.org/archive/43158.htm
- Peaceful Playgrounds offers a PDF titled "Benefits of Recess Before Lunch," which includes, in addition to the benefits, solutions to concerns and research citations. You'll find it here: https://www.peacefulplaygrounds.com/download/lunch/benefits-recess-before-lunch-facts.pdf
- Read this piece titled "Elementary School Students Forced to Eat Lunch in Complete Silence": https://www.sheknows.com/parenting/articles/1114267/texas-kids-forced-to-eat-lunch-in-silence/
- Action for Healthy Kids' "Time to Eat" offers steps you can take to advocate for longer lunch periods: https://www.actionforhealthykids.org/activity/time-to-eat/
- Read about a recent Harvard University study that determined kids don't get enough time to eat lunch here: https://philadelphia.cbslocal.com/2019/10/08/study-students-arent-getting-enough-time-to-eat-lunch/

Video

- Watch this video of a lunch period in an elementary school in Japan, and if you're so inclined, jot down the number of life lessons learned. I can assure you that your list will be long—and that everything on it will serve these students well, both in the present and in the future. You'll find it here: https://www.youtube.com/watch?v=hL5mKE4e4uU

Chapter 25

Articles

- For information on the impact of nature on health, check out the study "Measuring Connectedness to Nature in Preschool Children in an Urban Setting and Its Relation to Psychological Functioning": https://journals.plos.org/plosone/article?id=10.1371/journal.pone.0207057
- For information on the impact of nature on cognitive functioning, you can access a PDF of Nancy M. Well's study "At Home With Nature: Effects of 'Greenness' on Children's Cognitive Functioning" here: https://www.nrs.fs.fed.us/pubs/jrnl/2000/nc_2000_wells_001.pdf
- A PDF of "Coping With ADD: The Surprising Connection to Green Play Settings" can be accessed here: http://www.attitudematters.org/documents/Coping%20with%20ADD%20-%20Green%20Play%20Settings.pdf
- NAEYC offers an article titled "From Puddles to Pigeons: Learning About Nature in Cities" for those in urban settings. Access it here: https://www.naeyc.org/resources/pubs/yc/nov2018/learning-about-nature-cities

Books

- I strongly recommend Richard Louv's book, the full title of which is *Last Child in the Woods: Saving Our Children From Nature-Deficit Disorder*. I believe it's a must-read for everybody who cares about children.
- For a deeper dive, you might choose *Children in Nature: Psychological, Sociocultural, and Evolutionary Investigations*, edited by Peter H. Kahn Jr. and Stephen R. Kellert.

Podcast

- Listen to "What Is Nature Deficit? Why It Matters" here: https://www.bamradionetwork.com/track/what-is-nature-deficit-why-it-matters/

Chapter 26

Articles

- Dr. Peter Gray weighs in on "Risky Play: Why Children Love It and Need It": https://www.psychologytoday.com/us/blog/freedom-learn/201404/risky-play-why-children-love-it-and-need-it
- "How to Facilitate Risky Play in the Classroom" is a helpful article. You'll find it here: https://blog.himama.com/how-to-facilitate-risky-play/

Book

- Pediatric occupational therapist Angela Hanscom's book, *Balanced and Barefoot*, addresses risky play. You can read an excerpt here: https://www.washingtonpost.com/news/answer-sheet/wp/2016/07/04/why-some-risky-play-is-necessary-for-kids/

Podcasts

- Listen to "Risky Child's Play: The Good, the Bad, and the Mostly Good" on BAM!radio: https://www.bamradionetwork.com/track/risky-child-play-the-good-the-bad-and-the-ugly/
- You might also listen to "Are We Taking Playground Safety Too Far?": https://www.bamradionetwork.com/track/are-we-taking-playground-safety-too-far-2/

Chapter 27

Articles

- You can find the article "A Nation of Wimps" here: https://www.psychologytoday.com/us/articles/200411/nation-wimps

- Read "There's Never Been a Safer Time to Be a Kid in America": https://www.washingtonpost.com/news/wonk/wp/2015/04/14/theres-never-been-a-safer-time-to-be-a-kid-in-america/
- To quell fears regarding stranger danger, read "Five Myths About Missing Children": https://www.washingtonpost.com/opinions/five-myths-about-missing-children/2013/05/10/efee398c-b8b4-11e2-aa9e-a02b765ff0ea_story.html

Books

- *A Nation of Wimps* by Hara Estroff Marano is not only worth reading, but worth recommending to parents and decision makers.
- Read Frank Furedi's *How Fear Works* for a better understanding of fear's contagion.
- *Free-Range Kids: How to Raise Safe, Self-Reliant Children (Without Going Nuts With Worry)* by Lenore Skenazy is for parents but worth the time for teachers to read.
- Daniel Gardner's *The Science of Fear* offers another look at the contagion.

Organization

- Follow Let Grow (https://letgrow.org/) for myth-busting information.

Chapter 28

Articles

- The National Association of School Psychologists offers detailed guidance about conducting drills here: https://www.nasponline.org/resources-and-publications/resources-and-podcasts/school-climate-safety-and-crisis/systems-level-prevention/best-practice-considerations-for-schools-in-active-shooter-and-other-armed-assailant-drills
- You'll find an NPR piece titled "Experts Worry Active Shooter Drills in Schools Could Be Traumatic for Students" here: https://www.npr.org/2019/11/10/778015261/experts-worry-active-shooter-drills-in-schools-could-be-traumatic-for-students

- Launa Hall's piece can be found here: https://www
.washingtonpost.com/opinions/rehearsing-for-death-a-pre-
k-teacher-on-the-trouble-with-lockdown-drills/2014/10/28/
4ab456ea-5eb2-11e4-9f3a-7e28799e0549_story.html
- You can read Sergio Pecanha's piece here: https://
www.washingtonpost.com/opinions/2019/10/11/lockdown-
drills-an-american-quirk-out-control/?arc404=true.   This
article provides statistics offering some perspective on
the need for lockdown drills.
- *Education Week* offers "'I Worry Every Day': Lockdown
Drills Prompt Fear, Self-Reflection After School Shooting."
You can read it here: https://www.edweek.org/ew/articles/
2018/02/20/theyre-coming-for-me-and-my-kids.html

Podcast

- Listen to the BAM!radio podcast titled "Rehearsing for
Death: Shifting to Safety Drills That Do No Harm" here:
https://www.bamradionetwork.com/track/rehearsing-for-
death-shifting-to-safety-drills-that-do-no-harm/

Chapter 29
Article

- Read "The Role of Advocacy in Public Education," written by a teacher: https://www.advanc-ed.org/source/role-
advocacy-public-education

Miscellaneous

- NAEYC offers many resources regarding advocacy. You
can learn more here: https://www.naeyc.org/our-work/
public-policy-advocacy/build-your-advocacy-skills-and-
knowledge
- The McCormick Center for Early Childhood Leadership is
another great resource. Check out their "Early Childhood
Advocacy for Beginners" here: https://mccormickcenter.nl
.edu/library/early-childhood-advocacy-for-beginners-part-i/.

Chapter 30

Article

- Peter Gray's article, "K & Preschool Teachers: Last Stand in War on Childhood?," provides emotional support: https://www.psychologytoday.com/us/blog/freedom-learn/201507/k-preschool-teachers-last-stand-in-war-childhood?fbclid=IwAR0NbA-kYhDh7XLvMyjAgTJlHWFfvy2y4t24HPMwh4vTHlTQNq6DrFPBDc8

Podcast

- The 12-minute podcast, "ECE Advocacy 101: You're Either at the Table or on the Menu," offers lots of wonderful advice from the directors of four state AEYC organizations: http://www.bamradionetwork.com/naeyc-radio/1008-ece-advocacy-101-youre-either-at-the-table-or-on-the-menu

Video

- Watch the six-minute video called "5 Ways to Sneak Movement Into the Curriculum": https://www.youtube.com/watch?v=I1StHBuzoPs

Chapter 31

Miscellaneous

- Defending the Early Years offers an advocacy kit, as well as additional resources, here: https://dey.org/activists-tool-kit/
- Here's another early childhood advocacy toolkit: https://www.theounce.org/wp-content/uploads/2017/03/EarlyChildhoodAdvocacyToolkit.pdf
- You can learn about America for Early Ed here: http://www.americaforearlyed.org/
- You can learn about Resistbot here: https://resist.bot/

A SAGE Publishing Company

Helping educators make the greatest impact

CORWIN HAS ONE MISSION: to enhance education through intentional professional learning.

We build long-term relationships with our authors, educators, clients, and associations who partner with us to develop and continuously improve the best evidence-based practices that establish and support lifelong learning.

Solutions YOU WANT | Experts YOU TRUST | Results YOU NEED

EVENTS

>>> **INSTITUTES**

Corwin Institutes provide large regional events where educators collaborate with peers and learn from industry experts. Prepare to be recharged and motivated!

corwin.com/institutes

ON-SITE PD

>>> **ON-SITE PROFESSIONAL LEARNING**

Corwin on-site PD is delivered through high-energy keynotes, practical workshops, and custom coaching services designed to support knowledge development and implementation.

corwin.com/pd

>>> **PROFESSIONAL DEVELOPMENT RESOURCE CENTER**

The PD Resource Center provides school and district PD facilitators with the tools and resources needed to deliver effective PD.

corwin.com/pdrc

ONLINE

>>> **ADVANCE**

Designed for K–12 teachers, Advance offers a range of online learning options that can qualify for graduate-level credit and apply toward license renewal.

corwin.com/advance

Contact a PD Advisor at (800) 831-6640 or visit www.corwin.com for more information

CORWIN